ISBN 978-1-7348337-6-8

AF879343

LIFE180 Media
Attn: LIFE180
1801 W Azalea Dr
Chandler, AZ 85248

For ordering information or special discounts for bulk purchases, please contact LIFE180.

CHANGE
YOUR THINKING
CHANGE
YOUR ACTIONS
CHANGE
YOUR LIFE

LIFE180

AGENT SUCCESS PLANNER

LIFE180

AGENT SUCCESS PLANNER

You're holding in your hands the world's most effective planner for helping life insurance agents grow their business through personal growth, professional growth, activity management, and Living Intentionally for Excellence.

The planner has been inspired through my 15 years of experience in the life insurance, sales, and personal growth industries.

I am a big believer in Pearson's Law - "When performance is measured, performance improves. When performance is measured and reported back, the rate of improvement accelerates."

Sadly, when most people first enter the life insurance industry, they are on their own. They don't know where to start, what to measure, what to focus on for the fastest results, or how to balance their time.

What you are holding in your hands is the key to your success and fast growth.

I love the life insurance industry. I love how you have the ability to have a dramatic positive impact in the lives of everyone you come into contact with. I love how this business will stretch you and force you to become who you need to be to reach that next level of success for you.

If you want to differentiate yourself in the life insurance industry, you need to show up differently in the lives of the people you are trying to serve. This planner will be your day-to-day guide shepherding you on that path, helping you grow and help you show up more authentically to serve more people.

When I founded LIFE180, my wife and I developed that name because LIFE180 is actually two acronyms in one:

First: Leading Into Financial Excellence

Sadly most North American families are less than $400 per month away from bankruptcy. I believe our job as life insurance professionals is to show up differently to help them increase the efficiency in their financial life through better financial literacy and stewardship.

Second: Living Intentionally For Excellence

If you are not intentional about the life you want to create and the plan you have to get there, chances are you will start living for someone else's plan. If you want to create anything significant (which I hope you do), you need to be intentional about what you are doing to get there.

The 180 is simply about the sad reality that most people are not achieving the results they want in life - in almost every area.

As you use this planner every day, know that I didn't create it solely to help you sell more life insurance and make more money. All of that will happen as a byproduct of focus, intention, and activity in the right areas of life - simply by the added value you are contributing to the world.

I created this planner because I believe the world needs YOU to show up more powerfully in life. The world needs YOU to grow and be more intentional about how you choose to show up in the lives of others.

I hope you take this challenge seriously. Remember, people overestimate what they can accomplish in a year and underestimate what they can accomplish in a decade.

My promise to you is that if you truly engage with this challenge DAILY, you will achieve the daily growth that will help you become who you need to be to get to where you want to go.

Chris Kirkpatrick

Founder, LIFE180

Your Major Goals

this year

three year

five year

ten year

Major Projects

Major Events

Personal Improvement

50 People I am inspired to help this 90 days

Name / Phone and/or email		Name / Phone and/or email	
1		26	
2		27	
3		28	
4		29	
5		30	
6		31	
7		32	
8		33	
9		34	
10		35	
11		36	
12		37	
13		38	
14		39	
15		40	
16		41	
17		42	
18		43	
19		44	
20		45	
21		46	
22		47	
23		48	
24		49	
25		50	

Date __ / __ / __

Morning

Morning Mindset

The thing I am most excited about today is...

Something that might disrupt my success today is...

How I will deal with it...

A person who needs my help today is...

Someone I could surprise with an act of kindness today is...

Something I could do to demonstrate excellence or add true value to my community is...

One thing I could do to today that is out of my comfort zone is...

If I was a coach looking at my life, I would remind myself to remember that...

What is the one word I want to describe me as the best version of myself today?

I know today is a major success if...

Today's Top 3 Goals / Priorities

Morning Schedule		Point Value
5AM		
5:30		
6AM		
6:30		
7AM		
7:30		
8AM		
8:30		
9AM		
9:30		
10AM		
10:30		
11AM		

Daily Movement / Health

15 Point Day (Index of values for activities)

Make Appointment = 3 pts.
Have Meeting and schedule Follow Up = 3 pts.
Get Referral = 2 pts.
Application = 5 pts.
Policy Enforce = 5 pts.
Attend Network Event = 2pts.
Take Prospect/Client to Lunch/Event = 1 pt.
Send Affiliate Link to 5 People = 2 pts.
1 Hour of Reading or Education = 1 Pt.

Total Points

Afternoon

Tasks That Must be Completed

Who to connect with today

Afternoon Schedule

Point Value

12PM

12:30

1PM

1:30

2PM

2:30

3PM

3:30

4PM

4:30

5PM

5:30

6PM

Notes For Tomorrow / Appointments after 7PM

Daily Reflection

Something I truly appreciated about today was...

I am proud of the way I handled this task or situation today...

Something new I learned today was...
Today could have improved if I...

If I were my own coach, I would tell myself this about today...

Win The Day Scorecard

score yourself 1-5

Intention
I lived intentionally today according to my "why"

Energy
My physical and mental energy today

Boldness
Today I stepped out of my comfort zone in confidence and authenticity

Essentalism
I prioritized my day according to what mattered most to me

Influence
I made a positive impact on others today

Urgency
I am aware that if I don't help people, they may never be helped.

Date __ / __ / __

Morning

Morning Mindset

The thing I am most excited about today is...

Something that might disrupt my success today is...

How I will deal with it...

A person who needs my help today is...

Someone I could surprise with an act of kindness today is...

Something I could do to demonstrate excellence or add true value to my community is...

One thing I could do to today that is out of my comfort zone is...

If I was a coach looking at my life, I would remind myself to remember that...

What is the one word I want to describe me as the best version of myself today?

I know today is a major success if...

Today's Top 3 Goals / Priorities

Time	Morning Schedule	Point Value
5AM		
5:30		
6AM		
6:30		
7AM		
7:30		
8AM		
8:30		
9AM		
9:30		
10AM		
10:30		
11AM		

LIFE180

Daily Movement / Health

15 Point Day (Index of values for activities)

Make Appointment = 3 pts.
Have Meeting and schedule Follow Up = 3 pts.
Get Referral = 2 pts.
Application = 5 pts.
Policy Enforce = 5 pts.
Attend Network Event = 2pts.
Take Prospect/Client to Lunch/Event = 1 pt.
Send Affiliate Link to 5 People = 2 pts.
1 Hour of Reading or Education = 1 Pt.

Total Points

Afternoon

Tasks That Must be Completed

Who to connect with today

Afternoon Schedule

Point Value

12PM

12:30

1PM

1:30

2PM

2:30

3PM

3:30

4PM

4:30

5PM

5:30

6PM

Notes For Tomorrow / Appointments after 7PM

Daily Reflection

Something I truly appreciated about today was...

I am proud of the way I handled this task or situation today...

Something new I learned today was...
Today could have improved if I...

If I were my own coach, I would tell my-self this about today...

Win The Day Scorecard

score yourself 1-5

Intention
I lived intentionally today according to my "why"

Energy
My physical and mental energy today

Boldness
Today I stepped out of my comfort zone in confidence and authenticity

Essentalism
I prioritized my day according to what mattered most to me

Influence
I made a positive impact on others today

Urgency
I am aware that if I don't help people, they may never be helped.

Date __ / __ / __

Morning

Morning Mindset

The thing I am most excited about today is...

Something that might disrupt my success today is...

How I will deal with it...

A person who needs my help today is...

Someone I could surprise with an act of kindness today is...

Something I could do to demonstrate excellence or add true value to my community is...

One thing I could do to today that is out of my comfort zone is...

If I was a coach looking at my life, I would remind myself to remember that...

What is the one word I want to describe me as the best version of myself today?

I know today is a major success if...

Today's Top 3 Goals / Priorities

Morning Schedule		Point Value
5AM		
5:30		
6AM		
6:30		
7AM		
7:30		
8AM		
8:30		
9AM		
9:30		
10AM		
10:30		
11AM		

LIFE180

Daily Movement / Health

15 Point Day (Index of values for activities)

Make Appointment = 3 pts.
Have Meeting and schedule Follow Up = 3 pts.
Get Referral = 2 pts.
Application = 5 pts.
Policy Enforce = 5 pts.
Attend Network Event = 2pts.
Take Prospect/Client to Lunch/Event = 1 pt.
Send Affiliate Link to 5 People = 2 pts.
1 Hour of Reading or Education = 1 Pt.

Total Points

Afternoon

Tasks That Must be Completed

Afternoon Schedule

Point Value

12PM

12:30

1PM

1:30

2PM

2:30

3PM

3:30

4PM

4:30

5PM

5:30

6PM

Notes For Tomorrow / Appointments after 7PM

Who to connect with today

Daily Reflection

Something I truly appreciated about today was...

I am proud of the way I handled this task or situation today...

Something new I learned today was...
Today could have improved if I...

If I were my own coach, I would tell my-self this about today...

Win The Day Scorecard

score yourself 1-5

Intention
I lived intentionally today according to my "why"

Energy
My physical and mental energy today

Boldness
Today I stepped out of my comfort zone in confidence and authenticity

Essentalism
I prioritized my day according to what mattered most to me

Influence
I made a positive impact on others today

Urgency
I am aware that if I don't help people, they may never be helped.

Date __ / __ / __

Morning

Morning Mindset

The thing I am most excited about today is...

Something that might disrupt my success today is...

How I will deal with it...

A person who needs my help today is...

Someone I could surprise with an act of kindness today is...

Something I could do to demonstrate excellence or add true value to my community is...

One thing I could do to today that is out of my comfort zone is...

If I was a coach looking at my life, I would remind myself to remember that...

What is the one word I want to describe me as the best version of myself today?

I know today is a major success if...

Today's Top 3 Goals / Priorities

Morning Schedule		Point Value
5AM		
5:30		
6AM		
6:30		
7AM		
7:30		
8AM		
8:30		
9AM		
9:30		
10AM		
10:30		
11AM		

LIFE180

Daily Movement / Health

15 Point Day (Index of values for activities)

Make Appointment = 3 pts.
Have Meeting and schedule Follow Up = 3 pts.
Get Referral = 2 pts.
Application = 5 pts.
Policy Enforce = 5 pts.
Attend Network Event = 2pts.
Take Prospect/Client to Lunch/Event = 1 pt.
Send Affiliate Link to 5 People = 2 pts.
1 Hour of Reading or Education = 1 Pt.

Total Points

Afternoon

Tasks That Must be Completed

Who to connect with today

Afternoon Schedule

Point Value

12PM

12:30

1PM

1:30

2PM

2:30

3PM

3:30

4PM

4:30

5PM

5:30

6PM

Notes For Tomorrow / Appointments after 7PM

LIFE180

Daily Reflection

Something I truly appreciated about today was...

I am proud of the way I handled this task or situation today...

Something new I learned today was...

Today could have improved if I...

If I were my own coach, I would tell myself this about today...

Win The Day Scorecard

score yourself 1-5

Intention
I lived intentionally today according to my "why"

Energy
My physical and mental energy today

Boldness
Today I stepped out of my comfort zone in confidence and authenticity

Essentalism
I prioritized my day according to what mattered most to me

Influence
I made a positive impact on others today

Urgency
I am aware that if I don't help people, they may never be helped.

Date __ /__ / __

Morning

Morning Mindset

The thing I am most excited about today is...

Something that might disrupt my success today is...

How I will deal with it...

A person who needs my help today is...

Someone I could surprise with an act of kindness today is...

Something I could do to demonstrate excellence or add true value to my community is...

One thing I could do to today that is out of my comfort zone is...

If I was a coach looking at my life, I would remind myself to remember that...

What is the one word I want to describe me as the best version of myself today?

I know today is a major success if...

Today's Top 3 Goals / Priorities

Morning Schedule		Point Value
5AM		
5:30		
6AM		
6:30		
7AM		
7:30		
8AM		
8:30		
9AM		
9:30		
10AM		
10:30		
11AM		

LIFE180

Daily Movement / Health

15 Point Day (Index of values for activities)

Make Appointment = 3 pts.
Have Meeting and schedule Follow Up = 3 pts.
Get Referral = 2 pts.
Application = 5 pts.
Policy Enforce = 5 pts.
Attend Network Event = 2pts.
Take Prospect/Client to Lunch/Event = 1 pt.
Send Affiliate Link to 5 People = 2 pts.
1 Hour of Reading or Education = 1 Pt.

Total Points

Afternoon

Tasks That Must be Completed

Who to connect with today

Afternoon Schedule

Point Value

12PM

12:30

1PM

1:30

2PM

2:30

3PM

3:30

4PM

4:30

5PM

5:30

6PM

Notes For Tomorrow / Appointments after 7PM

LIFE180

Daily Reflection

Something I truly appreciated about today was...

I am proud of the way I handled this task or situation today...

Something new I learned today was...
Today could have improved if I...

If I were my own coach, I would tell myself this about today...

Win The Day Scorecard

score yourself 1-5

Intention
I lived intentionally today according to my "why"

Energy
My physical and mental energy today

Boldness
Today I stepped out of my comfort zone in confidence and authenticity

Essentialism
I prioritized my day according to what mattered most to me

Influence
I made a positive impact on others today

Urgency
I am aware that if I don't help people, they may never be helped.

Date __ / __ / __

Morning

Morning Mindset

The thing I am most excited about today is...

Something that might disrupt my success today is...

How I will deal with it...

A person who needs my help today is...

Someone I could surprise with an act of kindness today is...

Something I could do to demonstrate excellence or add true value to my community is...

One thing I could do to today that is out of my comfort zone is...

If I was a coach looking at my life, I would remind myself to remember that...

What is the one word I want to describe me as the best version of myself today?

I know today is a major success if...

Today's Top 3 Goals / Priorities

Morning Schedule		Point Value
5AM		
5:30		
6AM		
6:30		
7AM		
7:30		
8AM		
8:30		
9AM		
9:30		
10AM		
10:30		
11AM		

Daily Movement / Health

15 Point Day (Index of values for activities)

Make Appointment = 3 pts.
Have Meeting and schedule Follow Up = 3 pts.
Get Referral = 2 pts.
Application = 5 pts.
Policy Enforce = 5 pts.
Attend Network Event = 2pts.
Take Prospect/Client to Lunch/Event = 1 pt.
Send Affiliate Link to 5 People = 2 pts.
1 Hour of Reading or Education = 1 Pt.

Total Points

Afternoon

Tasks That Must be Completed

Afternoon Schedule

Point Value

12PM

12:30

1PM

1:30

2PM

2:30

3PM

3:30

4PM

4:30

5PM

5:30

6PM

Notes For Tomorrow / Appointments after 7PM

Who to connect with today

Daily Reflection

Something I truly appreciated about today was...

I am proud of the way I handled this task or situation today...

Something new I learned today was...

Today could have improved if I...

If I were my own coach, I would tell myself this about today...

Win The Day Scorecard

score yourself 1-5

Intention
I lived intentionally today according to my "why"

Energy
My physical and mental energy today

Boldness
Today I stepped out of my comfort zone in confidence and authenticity

Essentialism
I prioritized my day according to what mattered most to me

Influence
I made a positive impact on others today

Urgency
I am aware that if I don't help people, they may never be helped.

Date __ / __ / __

Morning

Morning Mindset

The thing I am most excited about today is...

Something that might disrupt my success today is...

How I will deal with it...

A person who needs my help today is...

Someone I could surprise with an act of kindness today is...

Something I could do to demonstrate excellence or add true value to my community is...

One thing I could do to today that is out of my comfort zone is...

If I was a coach looking at my life, I would remind myself to remember that...

What is the one word I want to describe me as the best version of myself today?

I know today is a major success if...

Today's Top 3 Goals / Priorities

Morning Schedule		Point Value
5AM		
5:30		
6AM		
6:30		
7AM		
7:30		
8AM		
8:30		
9AM		
9:30		
10AM		
10:30		
11AM		

LIFE180

Daily Movement / Health

15 Point Day (Index of values for activities)

Make Appointment = 3 pts.
Have Meeting and schedule Follow Up = 3 pts.
Get Referral = 2 pts.
Application = 5 pts.
Policy Enforce = 5 pts.
Attend Network Event = 2pts.
Take Prospect/Client to Lunch/Event = 1 pt.
Send Affiliate Link to 5 People = 2 pts.
1 Hour of Reading or Education = 1 Pt.

Total Points

Afternoon

Tasks That Must be Completed

Who to connect with today

Afternoon Schedule

Point Value

12PM

12:30

1PM

1:30

2PM

2:30

3PM

3:30

4PM

4:30

5PM

5:30

6PM

Notes For Tomorrow / Appointments after 7PM

Daily Reflection

Something I truly appreciated about today was...

I am proud of the way I handled this task or situation today...

Something new I learned today was...

Today could have improved if I...

If I were my own coach, I would tell my-self this about today...

Win The Day Scorecard

score yourself 1-5

Intention
I lived intentionally today according to my "why"

Energy
My physical and mental energy today

Boldness
Today I stepped out of my comfort zone in confidence and authenticity

Essentalism
I prioritized my day according to what mattered most to me

Influence
I made a positive impact on others today

Urgency
I am aware that if I don't help people, they may never be helped.

Weekly Learning Review

Three or more amazing things that happened this week

The main struggle I had this past week was...

If you were coaching yourself, how would you coach yourself to handle this next week?

Two areas I grew in this week were...

Three things I learned about others this week (your loved ones, friends, clients, etc...)

Something I could have done to have more success in the areas that matter to me was...

Weekly Win The Day Review

At the end of every day this past week, you scored yourself according to INTENTION, ENERGY, URGENCY, ESSENTIALISM, INFLUENCE, & BOLDNESS. Add the scores up for each section and include them in the bubbles below. Don't be hard on yourself, but be honest. Take your number and divide by 2. The maximum score you can receive is 105.

Intention	Energy	Essentialism
Urgency	**Influence**	**Boldness**

Total	

Dates: _ _ / _ _ / _ _ - _ _ / _ _ / _ _

Weekly Business Reflection

The area I excelled most in this week and why...

Something I could have done this past week to achieve more success...

What I will do differently next week to elevate my performance...

What is the one activity I am not doing enough of?

Who on the team can help me elevate my performance through joint work or mentoring?

Who on the team can I serve or collaborate with in a mutually beneficial way?

What am I most proud of this week?

If you were your own coach, what would you tell yourself you need to do next week to achieve your results?

Weekly Business Point Tracking

Day	Total Points
Monday	
Tuesday	
Wednesday	
Thursday	
Friday	
Saturday	
Sunday	
Total	

Date __ / __ / __

Morning

Morning Mindset

The thing I am most excited about today is...

Something that might disrupt my success today is...

How I will deal with it...

A person who needs my help today is...

Someone I could surprise with an act of kindness today is...

…nething I could do to demonstrate …llence or add true value to my …nunity is...

… I could do to today that is out of my comfort zone is...

If I was a coach looking at my life, I would remind myself to remember that...

What is the one word I want to describe me as the best version of myself today?

I know today is a major success if...

Today's Top 3 Goals / Priorities

Morning Schedule		Point Value
5AM		
5:30		
6AM		
6:30		
7AM		
7:30		
8AM		
8:30		
9AM		
9:30		
10AM		
10:30		
11AM		

Daily Movement / Health

15 Point Day (Index of values for activities)

Make Appointment = 3 pts.
Have Meeting and schedule Follow Up = 3 pts.
Get Referral = 2 pts.
Application = 5 pts.
Policy Enforce = 5 pts.
Attend Network Event = 2pts.
Take Prospect/Client to Lunch/Event = 1 pt.
Send Affiliate Link to 5 People = 2 pts.
1 Hour of Reading or Education = 1 Pt.

Total Points

Afternoon

Tasks That Must be Completed

Afternoon Schedule

Point Value

12PM

12:30

1PM

1:30

2PM

2:30

3PM

3:30

4PM

4:30

5PM

5:30

6PM

Notes For Tomorrow / Appointments after 7PM

Who to connect with today

Daily Reflection

Something I truly appreciated about today was...

I am proud of the way I handled this task or situation today...

Something new I learned today was...

Today could have improved if I...

If I were my own coach, I would tell myself this about today...

Win The Day Scorecard

score yourself 1-5

Intention
I lived intentionally today according to my "why"

Energy
My physical and mental energy today

Boldness
Today I stepped out of my comfort zone in confidence and authenticity

Essentalism
I prioritized my day according to what mattered most to me

Influence
I made a positive impact on others today

Urgency
I am aware that if I don't help people, they may never be helped.

Date __ / __ / __

Morning

Morning Mindset

The thing I am most excited about today is...

Something that might disrupt my success today is...

How I will deal with it...

A person who needs my help today is...

Someone I could surprise with an act of kindness today is...

Something I could do to demonstrate excellence or add true value to my community is...

One thing I could do to today that is out of my comfort zone is...

If I was a coach looking at my life, I would remind myself to remember that...

What is the one word I want to describe me as the best version of myself today?

I know today is a major success if...

Today's Top 3 Goals / Priorities

Morning Schedule		Point Value
5AM		
5:30		
6AM		
6:30		
7AM		
7:30		
8AM		
8:30		
9AM		
9:30		
10AM		
10:30		
11AM		

Daily Movement / Health

15 Point Day (Index of values for activities)

Make Appointment = 3 pts.
Have Meeting and schedule Follow Up = 3 pts.
Get Referral = 2 pts.
Application = 5 pts.
Policy Enforce = 5 pts.
Attend Network Event = 2pts.
Take Prospect/Client to Lunch/Event = 1 pt.
Send Affiliate Link to 5 People = 2 pts.
1 Hour of Reading or Education = 1 Pt.

Total Points

Afternoon

Tasks That Must be Completed

Who to connect with today

Afternoon Schedule

Point Value

12PM

12:30

1PM

1:30

2PM

2:30

3PM

3:30

4PM

4:30

5PM

5:30

6PM

Notes For Tomorrow / Appointments after 7PM

Daily Reflection

Something I truly appreciated about today was...

I am proud of the way I handled this task or situation today...

Something new I learned today was...

Today could have improved if I...

If I were my own coach, I would tell myself this about today...

Win The Day Scorecard

score yourself 1-5

Intention
I lived intentionally today according to my "why"

Energy
My physical and mental energy today

Boldness
Today I stepped out of my comfort zone in confidence and authenticity

Essentalism
I prioritized my day according to what mattered most to me

Influence
I made a positive impact on others today

Urgency
I am aware that if I don't help people, they may never be helped.

Date __ /__ / __

Morning

Morning Mindset

The thing I am most excited about today is...

Something that might disrupt my success today is...

How I will deal with it...

A person who needs my help today is...

Someone I could surprise with an act of kindness today is...

Something I could do to demonstrate excellence or add true value to my community is...

One thing I could do to today that is out of my comfort zone is...

If I was a coach looking at my life, I would remind myself to remember that...

What is the one word I want to describe me as the best version of myself today?

I know today is a major success if...

Today's Top 3 Goals / Priorities

Morning Schedule		Point Value
5AM		
5:30		
6AM		
6:30		
7AM		
7:30		
8AM		
8:30		
9AM		
9:30		
10AM		
10:30		
11AM		

LIFE180

Daily Movement / Health

15 Point Day (Index of values for activities)

Make Appointment = 3 pts.
Have Meeting and schedule Follow Up = 3 pts.
Get Referral = 2 pts.
Application = 5 pts.
Policy Enforce = 5 pts.
Attend Network Event = 2pts.
Take Prospect/Client to Lunch/Event = 1 pt.
Send Affiliate Link to 5 People = 2 pts.
1 Hour of Reading or Education = 1 Pt.

Total Points

Afternoon

Tasks That Must be Completed

Who to connect with today

Afternoon Schedule

Point Value

12PM

12:30

1PM

1:30

2PM

2:30

3PM

3:30

4PM

4:30

5PM

5:30

6PM

Notes For Tomorrow / Appointments after 7PM

Daily Reflection

Something I truly appreciated about today was...

I am proud of the way I handled this task or situation today...

Something new I learned today was...

Today could have improved if I...

If I were my own coach, I would tell myself this about today...

Win The Day Scorecard

score yourself 1-5

Intention
I lived intentionally today according to my "why"

Energy
My physical and mental energy today

Boldness
Today I stepped out of my comfort zone in confidence and authenticity

Essentalism
I prioritized my day according to what mattered most to me

Influence
I made a positive impact on others today

Urgency
I am aware that if I don't help people, they may never be helped.

Date __ / __ / __

Morning

Morning Mindset

The thing I am most excited about today is...

Something that might disrupt my success today is...

How I will deal with it...

A person who needs my help today is...

Someone I could surprise with an act of kindness today is...

Something I could do to demonstrate excellence or add true value to my community is...

One thing I could do to today that is out of my comfort zone is...

If I was a coach looking at my life, I would remind myself to remember that...

What is the one word I want to describe me as the best version of myself today?

I know today is a major success if...

Today's Top 3 Goals / Priorities

Morning Schedule		Point Value
5AM		
5:30		
6AM		
6:30		
7AM		
7:30		
8AM		
8:30		
9AM		
9:30		
10AM		
10:30		
11AM		

LIFE180

Daily Movement / Health

15 Point Day (Index of values for activities)

Make Appointment = 3 pts.
Have Meeting and schedule Follow Up = 3 pts.
Get Referral = 2 pts.
Application = 5 pts.
Policy Enforce = 5 pts.
Attend Network Event = 2pts.
Take Prospect/Client to Lunch/Event = 1 pt.
Send Affiliate Link to 5 People = 2 pts.
1 Hour of Reading or Education = 1 Pt.

Total Points

Afternoon

Tasks That Must be Completed

Who to connect with today

Afternoon Schedule

Point Value

12PM

12:30

1PM

1:30

2PM

2:30

3PM

3:30

4PM

4:30

5PM

5:30

6PM

Notes For Tomorrow / Appointments after 7PM

Daily Reflection

Something I truly appreciated about today was...

I am proud of the way I handled this task or situation today...

Something new I learned today was...

Today could have improved if I...

If I were my own coach, I would tell myself this about today...

Win The Day Scorecard

score yourself 1-5

Intention
I lived intentionally today according to my "why"

Energy
My physical and mental energy today

Boldness
Today I stepped out of my comfort zone in confidence and authenticity

Essentialism
I prioritized my day according to what mattered most to me

Influence
I made a positive impact on others today

Urgency
I am aware that if I don't help people, they may never be helped.

Date __ /__ / __

Morning

Morning Mindset

The thing I am most excited about today is...

Something that might disrupt my success today is...

How I will deal with it...

A person who needs my help today is...

Someone I could surprise with an act of kindness today is...

Something I could do to demonstrate excellence or add true value to my community is...

One thing I could do to today that is out of my comfort zone is...

If I was a coach looking at my life, I would remind myself to remember that...

What is the one word I want to describe me as the best version of myself today?

I know today is a major success if...

Today's Top 3 Goals / Priorities

Time	Morning Schedule	Point Value
5AM		
5:30		
6AM		
6:30		
7AM		
7:30		
8AM		
8:30		
9AM		
9:30		
10AM		
10:30		
11AM		

LIFE180

Daily Movement / Health

15 Point Day (Index of values for activities)

Make Appointment = 3 pts.
Have Meeting and schedule Follow Up = 3 pts.
Get Referral = 2 pts.
Application = 5 pts.
Policy Enforce = 5 pts.
Attend Network Event = 2pts.
Take Prospect/Client to Lunch/Event = 1 pt.
Send Affiliate Link to 5 People = 2 pts.
1 Hour of Reading or Education = 1 Pt.

Total Points

Afternoon

Tasks That Must be Completed

Afternoon Schedule

Point Value

12PM

12:30

1PM

1:30

2PM

2:30

3PM

3:30

4PM

4:30

5PM

5:30

6PM

Notes For Tomorrow / Appointments after 7PM

Who to connect with today

Daily Reflection

Something I truly appreciated about today was...

I am proud of the way I handled this task or situation today...

Something new I learned today was...

Today could have improved if I...

If I were my own coach, I would tell my-self this about today...

Win The Day Scorecard

score yourself 1-5

Intention
I lived intentionally today according to my "why"

Energy
My physical and mental energy today

Boldness
Today I stepped out of my comfort zone in confidence and authenticity

Essentialism
I prioritized my day according to what mattered most to me

Influence
I made a positive impact on others today

Urgency
I am aware that if I don't help people, they may never be helped.

Date __ / __ / __

Morning

Morning Mindset

The thing I am most excited about today is...

Something that might disrupt my success today is...

How I will deal with it...

A person who needs my help today is...

Someone I could surprise with an act of kindness today is...

Something I could do to demonstrate excellence or add true value to my community is...

One thing I could do to today that is out of my comfort zone is...

If I was a coach looking at my life, I would remind myself to remember that...

What is the one word I want to describe me as the best version of myself today?

I know today is a major success if...

Today's Top 3 Goals / Priorities

Morning Schedule		Point Value
5AM		
5:30		
6AM		
6:30		
7AM		
7:30		
8AM		
8:30		
9AM		
9:30		
10AM		
10:30		
11AM		

LIFE180

Daily Movement / Health

15 Point Day (Index of values for activities)

Make Appointment = 3 pts.
Have Meeting and schedule Follow Up = 3 pts.
Get Referral = 2 pts.
Application = 5 pts.
Policy Enforce = 5 pts.
Attend Network Event = 2pts.
Take Prospect/Client to Lunch/Event = 1 pt.
Send Affiliate Link to 5 People = 2 pts.
1 Hour of Reading or Education = 1 Pt.

Total Points

Afternoon

Tasks That Must be Completed

Who to connect with today

Afternoon Schedule

Point Value

12PM

12:30

1PM

1:30

2PM

2:30

3PM

3:30

4PM

4:30

5PM

5:30

6PM

Daily Reflection

Something I truly appreciated about today was...

I am proud of the way I handled this task or situation today...

Something new I learned today was...

Today could have improved if I...

If I were my own coach, I would tell myself this about today...

Notes For Tomorrow / Appointments after 7PM

Win The Day Scorecard

score yourself 1-5

Intention
I lived intentionally today according to my "why"

Energy
My physical and mental energy today

Boldness
Today I stepped out of my comfort zone in confidence and authenticity

Essentalism
I prioritized my day according to what mattered most to me

Influence
I made a positive impact on others today

Urgency
I am aware that if I don't help people, they may never be helped.

Date __ / __ / __

Morning

Morning Mindset

The thing I am most excited about today is...

Something that might disrupt my success today is...

How I will deal with it...

A person who needs my help today is...

Someone I could surprise with an act of kindness today is...

Something I could do to demonstrate excellence or add true value to my community is...

One thing I could do to today that is out of my comfort zone is...

If I was a coach looking at my life, I would remind myself to remember that...

What is the one word I want to describe me as the best version of myself today?

I know today is a major success if...

Today's Top 3 Goals / Priorities

Morning Schedule		Point Value
5AM		
5:30		
6AM		
6:30		
7AM		
7:30		
8AM		
8:30		
9AM		
9:30		
10AM		
10:30		
11AM		

LIFE180

Daily Movement / Health

15 Point Day (Index of values for activities)

Make Appointment = 3 pts.
Have Meeting and schedule Follow Up = 3 pts.
Get Referral = 2 pts.
Application = 5 pts.
Policy Enforce = 5 pts.
Attend Network Event = 2pts.
Take Prospect/Client to Lunch/Event = 1 pt.
Send Affiliate Link to 5 People = 2 pts.
1 Hour of Reading or Education = 1 Pt.

Total Points

Afternoon

Tasks That Must be Completed

Who to connect with today

Afternoon Schedule

Point Value

12PM

12:30

1PM

1:30

2PM

2:30

3PM

3:30

4PM

4:30

5PM

5:30

6PM

Notes For Tomorrow / Appointments after 7PM

Daily Reflection

Something I truly appreciated about today was...

I am proud of the way I handled this task or situation today...

Something new I learned today was...

Today could have improved if I...

If I were my own coach, I would tell myself this about today...

Win The Day Scorecard

score yourself 1-5

Intention
I lived intentionally today according to my "why"

Energy
My physical and mental energy today

Boldness
Today I stepped out of my comfort zone in confidence and authenticity

Essentalism
I prioritized my day according to what mattered most to me

Influence
I made a positive impact on others today

Urgency
I am aware that if I don't help people, they may never be helped.

Weekly Learning Review

Three or more amazing things that happened this week

The main struggle I had this past week was...

If you were coaching yourself, how would you coach yourself to handle this next week?

Two areas I grew in this week were...

Three things I learned about others this week (your loved ones, friends, clients, etc...)

Something I could have done to have more success in the areas that matter to me was...

Weekly Win The Day Review

At the end of every day this past week, you scored yourself according to INTENTION, ENERGY, URGENCY, ESSENTIALISM, INFLUENCE, & BOLDNESS. Add the scores up for each section and include them in the bubbles below. Don't be hard on yourself, but be honest. Take your number and divide by 2. The maximum score you can receive is 105.

Intention	Energy	Essentialism
Urgency	**Influence**	**Boldness**

Dates: _ _ / _ _ / _ _ - _ _ / _ _ / _ _

Total	

Weekly Business Reflection

The area I excelled most in this week and why...

Something I could have done this past week to achieve more success...

What I will do differently next week to elevate my performance...

What is the one activity I am not doing enough of?

Who on the team can help me elevate my performance through joint work or mentoring?

Who on the team can I serve or collaborate with in a mutually beneficial way?

What am I most proud of this week?

If you were your own coach, what would you tell yourself you need to do next week to achieve your results?

Weekly Business Point Tracking

Day	Total Points
Monday	
Tuesday	
Wednesday	
Thursday	
Friday	
Saturday	
Sunday	
Total	

Date __ / __ / __

Morning

Morning Mindset

The thing I am most excited about today is...

Something that might disrupt my success today is...

How I will deal with it...

A person who needs my help today is...

Someone I could surprise with an act of kindness today is...

Something I could do to demonstrate excellence or add true value to my community is...

One thing I could do to today that is out of my comfort zone is...

If I was a coach looking at my life, I would remind myself to remember that...

What is the one word I want to describe me as the best version of myself today?

I know today is a major success if...

Today's Top 3 Goals / Priorities

Morning Schedule		Point Value
5AM		
5:30		
6AM		
6:30		
7AM		
7:30		
8AM		
8:30		
9AM		
9:30		
10AM		
10:30		
11AM		

LIFE180

Daily Movement / Health

15 Point Day (Index of values for activities)

Make Appointment = 3 pts.
Have Meeting and schedule Follow Up = 3 pts.
Get Referral = 2 pts.
Application = 5 pts.
Policy Enforce = 5 pts.
Attend Network Event = 2pts.
Take Prospect/Client to Lunch/Event = 1 pt.
Send Affiliate Link to 5 People = 2 pts.
1 Hour of Reading or Education = 1 Pt.

Total Points

Afternoon

Tasks That Must be Completed

Who to connect with today

Afternoon Schedule

Point Value

12PM

12:30

1PM

1:30

2PM

2:30

3PM

3:30

4PM

4:30

5PM

5:30

6PM

Notes For Tomorrow / Appointments after 7PM

Daily Reflection

Something I truly appreciated about today was...

I am proud of the way I handled this task or situation today...

Something new I learned today was...

Today could have improved if I...

If I were my own coach, I would tell my-self this about today...

Win The Day Scorecard

score yourself 1-5

Intention
I lived intentionally today according to my "why"

Energy
My physical and mental energy today

Boldness
Today I stepped out of my comfort zone in confidence and authenticity

Essentialism
I prioritized my day according to what mattered most to me

Influence
I made a positive impact on others today

Urgency
I am aware that if I don't help people, they may never be helped.

Date __ /__ / __

Morning

Morning Mindset

The thing I am most excited about today is...

Something that might disrupt my success today is...

How I will deal with it...

A person who needs my help today is...

Someone I could surprise with an act of kindness today is...

Something I could do to demonstrate excellence or add true value to my community is...

One thing I could do to today that is out of my comfort zone is...

If I was a coach looking at my life, I would remind myself to remember that...

What is the one word I want to describe me as the best version of myself today?

I know today is a major success if...

Today's Top 3 Goals / Priorities

Morning Schedule		Point Value
5AM		
5:30		
6AM		
6:30		
7AM		
7:30		
8AM		
8:30		
9AM		
9:30		
10AM		
10:30		
11AM		

LIFE 180

Daily Movement / Health

15 Point Day (Index of values for activities)

Make Appointment = 3 pts.
Have Meeting and schedule Follow Up = 3 pts.
Get Referral = 2 pts.
Application = 5 pts.
Policy Enforce = 5 pts.
Attend Network Event = 2pts.
Take Prospect/Client to Lunch/Event = 1 pt.
Send Affiliate Link to 5 People = 2 pts.
1 Hour of Reading or Education = 1 Pt.

Total Points

Afternoon

Tasks That Must be Completed

Who to connect with today

Afternoon Schedule

Point Value

12PM

12:30

1PM

1:30

2PM

2:30

3PM

3:30

4PM

4:30

5PM

5:30

6PM

Notes For Tomorrow / Appointments after 7PM

LIFE180

Daily Reflection

Something I truly appreciated about today was...

I am proud of the way I handled this task or situation today...

Something new I learned today was...

Today could have improved if I...

If I were my own coach, I would tell myself this about today...

Win The Day Scorecard

score yourself 1-5

Intention
I lived intentionally today according to my "why"

Energy
My physical and mental energy today

Boldness
Today I stepped out of my comfort zone in confidence and authenticity

Essentalism
I prioritized my day according to what mattered most to me

Influence
I made a positive impact on others today

Urgency
I am aware that if I don't help people, they may never be helped.

Date __ / __ / __

Morning

Morning Mindset

The thing I am most excited about today is...

Something that might disrupt my success today is...

How I will deal with it...

A person who needs my help today is...

Someone I could surprise with an act of kindness today is...

Something I could do to demonstrate excellence or add true value to my community is...

One thing I could do to today that is out of my comfort zone is...

If I was a coach looking at my life, I would remind myself to remember that...

What is the one word I want to describe me as the best version of myself today?

I know today is a major success if...

Today's Top 3 Goals / Priorities

Morning Schedule		Point Value
5AM		
5:30		
6AM		
6:30		
7AM		
7:30		
8AM		
8:30		
9AM		
9:30		
10AM		
10:30		
11AM		

LIFE180

Daily Movement / Health

15 Point Day (Index of values for activities)

Make Appointment = 3 pts.
Have Meeting and schedule Follow Up = 3 pts.
Get Referral = 2 pts.
Application = 5 pts.
Policy Enforce = 5 pts.
Attend Network Event = 2pts.
Take Prospect/Client to Lunch/Event = 1 pt.
Send Affiliate Link to 5 People = 2 pts.
1 Hour of Reading or Education = 1 Pt.

Total Points

Afternoon

Tasks That Must be Completed

Who to connect with today

Afternoon Schedule

Point Value

12PM

12:30

1PM

1:30

2PM

2:30

3PM

3:30

4PM

4:30

5PM

5:30

6PM

Notes For Tomorrow / Appointments after 7PM

Daily Reflection

Something I truly appreciated about today was...

I am proud of the way I handled this task or situation today...

Something new I learned today was...
Today could have improved if I...

If I were my own coach, I would tell myself this about today...

Win The Day Scorecard

score yourself 1-5

Intention
I lived intentionally today according to my "why"

Energy
My physical and mental energy today

Boldness
Today I stepped out of my comfort zone in confidence and authenticity

Essentialism
I prioritized my day according to what mattered most to me

Influence
I made a positive impact on others today

Urgency
I am aware that if I don't help people, they may never be helped.

Date __ /__ / __

Morning

Morning Mindset

The thing I am most excited about today is...

Something that might disrupt my success today is...

How I will deal with it...

A person who needs my help today is...

Someone I could surprise with an act of kindness today is...

Something I could do to demonstrate excellence or add true value to my community is...

One thing I could do to today that is out of my comfort zone is...

If I was a coach looking at my life, I would remind myself to remember that...

What is the one word I want to describe me as the best version of myself today?

I know today is a major success if...

Today's Top 3 Goals / Priorities

Morning Schedule		Point Value
5AM		
5:30		
6AM		
6:30		
7AM		
7:30		
8AM		
8:30		
9AM		
9:30		
10AM		
10:30		
11AM		

Daily Movement / Health

15 Point Day (Index of values for activities)

Make Appointment = 3 pts.
Have Meeting and schedule Follow Up = 3 pts.
Get Referral = 2 pts.
Application = 5 pts.
Policy Enforce = 5 pts.
Attend Network Event = 2pts.
Take Prospect/Client to Lunch/Event = 1 pt.
Send Affiliate Link to 5 People = 2 pts.
1 Hour of Reading or Education = 1 Pt.

Total Points

Afternoon

Tasks That Must be Completed

Afternoon Schedule

Point Value

12PM

12:30

1PM

1:30

2PM

2:30

3PM

3:30

4PM

4:30

5PM

5:30

6PM

Notes For Tomorrow / Appointments after 7PM

Who to connect with today

Daily Reflection

Something I truly appreciated about today was...

I am proud of the way I handled this task or situation today...

Something new I learned today was...
Today could have improved if I...

If I were my own coach, I would tell myself this about today...

Win The Day Scorecard

score yourself 1-5

Intention
I lived intentionally today according to my "why"

Energy
My physical and mental energy today

Boldness
Today I stepped out of my comfort zone in confidence and authenticity

Essentalism
I prioritized my day according to what mattered most to me

Influence
I made a positive impact on others today

Urgency
I am aware that if I don't help people, they may never be helped.

Date __ / __ / __

Morning

Morning Mindset

The thing I am most excited about today is...

Something that might disrupt my success today is...

How I will deal with it...

A person who needs my help today is...

Someone I could surprise with an act of kindness today is...

Something I could do to demonstrate excellence or add true value to my community is...

One thing I could do to today that is out of my comfort zone is...

If I was a coach looking at my life, I would remind myself to remember that...

What is the one word I want to describe me as the best version of myself today?

I know today is a major success if...

Today's Top 3 Goals / Priorities

	Morning Schedule	Point Value
5AM		
5:30		
6AM		
6:30		
7AM		
7:30		
8AM		
8:30		
9AM		
9:30		
10AM		
10:30		
11AM		

LIFE180

Daily Movement / Health

15 Point Day (Index of values for activities)

Make Appointment = 3 pts.
Have Meeting and schedule Follow Up = 3 pts.
Get Referral = 2 pts.
Application = 5 pts.
Policy Enforce = 5 pts.
Attend Network Event = 2pts.
Take Prospect/Client to Lunch/Event = 1 pt.
Send Affiliate Link to 5 People = 2 pts.
1 Hour of Reading or Education = 1 Pt.

Total Points

Afternoon

Tasks That Must be Completed

Who to connect with today

Afternoon Schedule

Point Value

12PM

12:30

1PM

1:30

2PM

2:30

3PM

3:30

4PM

4:30

5PM

5:30

6PM

Notes For Tomorrow / Appointments after 7PM

Daily Reflection

Something I truly appreciated about today was...

I am proud of the way I handled this task or situation today...

Something new I learned today was...

Today could have improved if I...

If I were my own coach, I would tell myself this about today...

Win The Day Scorecard

score yourself 1-5

Intention
I lived intentionally today according to my "why"

Energy
My physical and mental energy today

Boldness
Today I stepped out of my comfort zone in confidence and authenticity

Essentalism
I prioritized my day according to what mattered most to me

Influence
I made a positive impact on others today

Urgency
I am aware that if I don't help people, they may never be helped.

Date __ / __ / __

Morning

Morning Mindset

The thing I am most excited about today is...

Something that might disrupt my success today is...

How I will deal with it...

A person who needs my help today is...

Someone I could surprise with an act of kindness today is...

Something I could do to demonstrate excellence or add true value to my community is...

One thing I could do to today that is out of my comfort zone is...

If I was a coach looking at my life, I would remind myself to remember that...

What is the one word I want to describe me as the best version of myself today?

I know today is a major success if...

Today's Top 3 Goals / Priorities

Morning Schedule		Point Value
5AM		
5:30		
6AM		
6:30		
7AM		
7:30		
8AM		
8:30		
9AM		
9:30		
10AM		
10:30		
11AM		

LIFE180

Daily Movement / Health

15 Point Day (Index of values for activities)

Make Appointment = 3 pts.
Have Meeting and schedule Follow Up = 3 pts.
Get Referral = 2 pts.
Application = 5 pts.
Policy Enforce = 5 pts.
Attend Network Event = 2pts.
Take Prospect/Client to Lunch/Event = 1 pt.
Send Affiliate Link to 5 People = 2 pts.
1 Hour of Reading or Education = 1 Pt.

Total Points

Afternoon

Tasks That Must be Completed

Who to connect with today

Afternoon Schedule

Point Value

12PM

12:30

1PM

1:30

2PM

2:30

3PM

3:30

4PM

4:30

5PM

5:30

6PM

Notes For Tomorrow / Appointments after 7PM

Daily Reflection

Something I truly appreciated about today was...

I am proud of the way I handled this task or situation today...

Something new I learned today was...

Today could have improved if I...

If I were my own coach, I would tell myself this about today...

Win The Day Scorecard

score yourself 1-5

Intention
I lived intentionally today according to my "why"

Energy
My physical and mental energy today

Boldness
Today I stepped out of my comfort zone in confidence and authenticity

Essentalism
I prioritized my day according to what mattered most to me

Influence
I made a positive impact on others today

Urgency
I am aware that if I don't help people, they may never be helped.

Date __ / __ / __

Morning

Morning Mindset

The thing I am most excited about today is...

Something that might disrupt my success today is...

How I will deal with it...

A person who needs my help today is...

Someone I could surprise with an act of kindness today is...

Something I could do to demonstrate excellence or add true value to my community is...

One thing I could do to today that is out of my comfort zone is...

If I was a coach looking at my life, I would remind myself to remember that...

What is the one word I want to describe me as the best version of myself today?

I know today is a major success if...

Today's Top 3 Goals / Priorities

Time	Morning Schedule	Point Value
5AM		
5:30		
6AM		
6:30		
7AM		
7:30		
8AM		
8:30		
9AM		
9:30		
10AM		
10:30		
11AM		

Daily Movement / Health

15 Point Day (Index of values for activities)

Make Appointment = 3 pts.
Have Meeting and schedule Follow Up = 3 pts.
Get Referral = 2 pts.
Application = 5 pts.
Policy Enforce = 5 pts.
Attend Network Event = 2pts.
Take Prospect/Client to Lunch/Event = 1 pt.
Send Affiliate Link to 5 People = 2 pts.
1 Hour of Reading or Education = 1 Pt.

Total Points

Afternoon

Tasks That Must be Completed

Who to connect with today

Afternoon Schedule

Point Value

12PM

12:30

1PM

1:30

2PM

2:30

3PM

3:30

4PM

4:30

5PM

5:30

6PM

Notes For Tomorrow / Appointments after 7PM

Daily Reflection

Something I truly appreciated about today was...

I am proud of the way I handled this task or situation today...

Something new I learned today was...
Today could have improved if I...

If I were my own coach, I would tell my-self this about today...

Win The Day Scorecard

score yourself 1-5

Intention
I lived intentionally today according to my "why"

Energy
My physical and mental energy today

Boldness
Today I stepped out of my comfort zone in confidence and authenticity

Essentialism
I prioritized my day according to what mattered most to me

Influence
I made a positive impact on others today

Urgency
I am aware that if I don't help people, they may never be helped.

Weekly Learning Review

Three or more amazing things that happened this week

The main struggle I had this past week was...

If you were coaching yourself, how would you coach yourself to handle this next week?

Two areas I grew in this week were...

Three things I learned about others this week (your loved ones, friends, clients, etc...)

Something I could have done to have more success in the areas that matter to me was...

Weekly Win The Day Review

At the end of every day this past week, you scored yourself according to INTENTION, ENERGY, URGENCY, ESSENTIALISM, INFLUENCE, & BOLDNESS. Add the scores up for each section and include them in the bubbles below. Don't be hard on yourself, but be honest. Take your number and divide by 2. The maximum score you can receive is 105.

Intention	Energy	Essentialism
Urgency	**Influence**	**Boldness**

Dates: _ _ / _ _ / _ _ - _ _ / _ _ / _ _

Total	

Weekly Business Reflection

The area I excelled most in this week and why...

Something I could have done this past week to achieve more success...

What I will do differently next week to elevate my performance...

What is the one activity I am not doing enough of?

Who on the team can help me elevate my performance through joint work or mentoring?

Who on the team can I serve or collaborate with in a mutually beneficial way?

What am I most proud of this week?

If you were your own coach, what would you tell yourself you need to do next week to achieve your results?

Weekly Business Point Tracking

Day	Total Points
Monday	
Tuesday	
Wednesday	
Thursday	
Friday	
Saturday	
Sunday	
Total	

Date __ / __ / __

Morning

Morning Mindset

The thing I am most excited about today is...

Something that might disrupt my success today is...

How I will deal with it...

A person who needs my help today is...

Someone I could surprise with an act of kindness today is...

Something I could do to demonstrate excellence or add true value to my community is...

One thing I could do to today that is out of my comfort zone is...

If I was a coach looking at my life, I would remind myself to remember that...

What is the one word I want to describe me as the best version of myself today?

I know today is a major success if...

Today's Top 3 Goals / Priorities

Time	Morning Schedule	Point Value
5AM		
5:30		
6AM		
6:30		
7AM		
7:30		
8AM		
8:30		
9AM		
9:30		
10AM		
10:30		
11AM		

Daily Movement / Health

15 Point Day (Index of values for activities)

Make Appointment = 3 pts.
Have Meeting and schedule Follow Up = 3 pts.
Get Referral = 2 pts.
Application = 5 pts.
Policy Enforce = 5 pts.
Attend Network Event = 2pts.
Take Prospect/Client to Lunch/Event = 1 pt.
Send Affiliate Link to 5 People = 2 pts.
1 Hour of Reading or Education = 1 Pt.

Total Points

Afternoon

Tasks That Must be Completed

Who to connect with today

Afternoon Schedule | Point Value

12PM

12:30

1PM

1:30

2PM

2:30

3PM

3:30

4PM

4:30

5PM

5:30

6PM

Notes For Tomorrow / Appointments after 7PM

Daily Reflection

Something I truly appreciated about today was...

I am proud of the way I handled this task or situation today...

Something new I learned today was...
Today could have improved if I...

If I were my own coach, I would tell myself this about today...

Win The Day Scorecard

score yourself 1-5

Intention
I lived intentionally today according to my "why"

Energy
My physical and mental energy today

Boldness
Today I stepped out of my comfort zone in confidence and authenticity

Essentalism
I prioritized my day according to what mattered most to me

Influence
I made a positive impact on others today

Urgency
I am aware that if I don't help people, they may never be helped.

Date __ /__ / __

Morning

Morning Mindset

The thing I am most excited about today is...

Something that might disrupt my success today is...

How I will deal with it...

A person who needs my help today is...

Someone I could surprise with an act of kindness today is...

Something I could do to demonstrate excellence or add true value to my community is...

One thing I could do to today that is out of my comfort zone is...

If I was a coach looking at my life, I would remind myself to remember that...

What is the one word I want to describe me as the best version of myself today?

I know today is a major success if...

Today's Top 3 Goals / Priorities

	Morning Schedule	Point Value
5AM		
5:30		
6AM		
6:30		
7AM		
7:30		
8AM		
8:30		
9AM		
9:30		
10AM		
10:30		
11AM		

LIFE180

Daily Movement / Health

15 Point Day (Index of values for activities)

Make Appointment = 3 pts.
Have Meeting and schedule Follow Up = 3 pts.
Get Referral = 2 pts.
Application = 5 pts.
Policy Enforce = 5 pts.
Attend Network Event = 2pts.
Take Prospect/Client to Lunch/Event = 1 pt.
Send Affiliate Link to 5 People = 2 pts.
1 Hour of Reading or Education = 1 Pt.

Total Points

Afternoon

Tasks That Must be Completed

Who to connect with today

Afternoon Schedule

Point Value

12PM

12:30

1PM

1:30

2PM

2:30

3PM

3:30

4PM

4:30

5PM

5:30

6PM

Daily Reflection

Something I truly appreciated about today was...

I am proud of the way I handled this task or situation today...

Something new I learned today was...
Today could have improved if I...

If I were my own coach, I would tell myself this about today...

Win The Day Scorecard

score yourself 1-5

Intention
I lived intentionally today according to my "why"

Energy
My physical and mental energy today

Boldness
Today I stepped out of my comfort zone in confidence and authenticity

Essentalism
I prioritized my day according to what mattered most to me

Influence
I made a positive impact on others today

Urgency
I am aware that if I don't help people, they may never be helped.

Notes For Tomorrow / Appointments after 7PM

Date __ / __ / __

Morning

Morning Mindset

The thing I am most excited about today is...

Something that might disrupt my success today is...

How I will deal with it...

A person who needs my help today is...

Someone I could surprise with an act of kindness today is...

Something I could do to demonstrate excellence or add true value to my community is...

One thing I could do to today that is out of my comfort zone is...

If I was a coach looking at my life, I would remind myself to remember that...

What is the one word I want to describe me as the best version of myself today?

I know today is a major success if...

Daily Movement / Health

Today's Top 3 Goals / Priorities

Morning Schedule		Point Value
5AM		
5:30		
6AM		
6:30		
7AM		
7:30		
8AM		
8:30		
9AM		
9:30		
10AM		
10:30		
11AM		

15 Point Day (Index of values for activities)

Make Appointment = 3 pts.
Have Meeting and schedule Follow Up = 3 pts.
Get Referral = 2 pts.
Application = 5 pts.
Policy Enforce = 5 pts.
Attend Network Event = 2pts.
Take Prospect/Client to Lunch/Event = 1 pt.
Send Affiliate Link to 5 People = 2 pts.
1 Hour of Reading or Education = 1 Pt.

Total Points

Afternoon

Tasks That Must be Completed

Who to connect with today

Afternoon Schedule

Point Value

12PM

12:30

1PM

1:30

2PM

2:30

3PM

3:30

4PM

4:30

5PM

5:30

6PM

Notes For Tomorrow / Appointments after 7PM

Daily Reflection

Something I truly appreciated about today was...

I am proud of the way I handled this task or situation today...

Something new I learned today was...
Today could have improved if I...

If I were my own coach, I would tell myself this about today...

Win The Day Scorecard

score yourself 1-5

Intention
I lived intentionally today according to my "why"

Energy
My physical and mental energy today

Boldness
Today I stepped out of my comfort zone in confidence and authenticity

Essentalism
I prioritized my day according to what mattered most to me

Influence
I made a positive impact on others today

Urgency
I am aware that if I don't help people, they may never be helped.

Date __ /__ / __

Morning

Morning Mindset

The thing I am most excited about today is...

Something that might disrupt my success today is...

How I will deal with it...

A person who needs my help today is...

Someone I could surprise with an act of kindness today is...

Something I could do to demonstrate excellence or add true value to my community is...

One thing I could do to today that is out of my comfort zone is...

If I was a coach looking at my life, I would remind myself to remember that...

What is the one word I want to describe me as the best version of myself today?

I know today is a major success if...

Today's Top 3 Goals / Priorities

Morning Schedule		Point Value
5AM		
5:30		
6AM		
6:30		
7AM		
7:30		
8AM		
8:30		
9AM		
9:30		
10AM		
10:30		
11AM		

Daily Movement / Health

15 Point Day (Index of values for activities)

Make Appointment = 3 pts.
Have Meeting and schedule Follow Up = 3 pts.
Get Referral = 2 pts.
Application = 5 pts.
Policy Enforce = 5 pts.
Attend Network Event = 2pts.
Take Prospect/Client to Lunch/Event = 1 pt.
Send Affiliate Link to 5 People = 2 pts.
1 Hour of Reading or Education = 1 Pt.

Total Points

Afternoon

Tasks That Must be Completed

Who to connect with today

Afternoon Schedule

Point Value

12PM
12:30
1PM
1:30
2PM
2:30
3PM
3:30
4PM
4:30
5PM
5:30
6PM

Notes For Tomorrow / Appointments after 7PM

LIFE180

Daily Reflection

Something I truly appreciated about today was...

I am proud of the way I handled this task or situation today...

Something new I learned today was...
Today could have improved if I...

If I were my own coach, I would tell myself this about today...

Win The Day Scorecard

score yourself 1-5

Intention
I lived intentionally today according to my "why"

Energy
My physical and mental energy today

Boldness
Today I stepped out of my comfort zone in confidence and authenticity

Essentalism
I prioritized my day according to what mattered most to me

Influence
I made a positive impact on others today

Urgency
I am aware that if I don't help people, they may never be helped.

Date __ /__ / __

Morning

Morning Mindset

The thing I am most excited about today is...

Something that might disrupt my success today is...

How I will deal with it...

A person who needs my help today is...

Someone I could surprise with an act of kindness today is...

Something I could do to demonstrate excellence or add true value to my community is...

One thing I could do to today that is out of my comfort zone is...

If I was a coach looking at my life, I would remind myself to remember that...

What is the one word I want to describe me as the best version of myself today?

I know today is a major success if...

Today's Top 3 Goals / Priorities

Morning Schedule		Point Value
5AM		
5:30		
6AM		
6:30		
7AM		
7:30		
8AM		
8:30		
9AM		
9:30		
10AM		
10:30		
11AM		

LIFE180

Daily Movement / Health

15 Point Day (Index of values for activities)

Make Appointment = 3 pts.
Have Meeting and schedule Follow Up = 3 pts.
Get Referral = 2 pts.
Application = 5 pts.
Policy Enforce = 5 pts.
Attend Network Event = 2pts.
Take Prospect/Client to Lunch/Event = 1 pt.
Send Affiliate Link to 5 People = 2 pts.
1 Hour of Reading or Education = 1 Pt.

Total Points

Afternoon

Tasks That Must be Completed

Who to connect with today

Afternoon Schedule

Point Value

12PM

12:30

1PM

1:30

2PM

2:30

3PM

3:30

4PM

4:30

5PM

5:30

6PM

Notes For Tomorrow / Appointments after 7PM

Daily Reflection

Something I truly appreciated about today was...

I am proud of the way I handled this task or situation today...

Something new I learned today was...
Today could have improved if I...

If I were my own coach, I would tell my-self this about today...

Win The Day Scorecard

score yourself 1-5

Intention
I lived intentionally today according to my "why"

Energy
My physical and mental energy today

Boldness
Today I stepped out of my comfort zone in confidence and authenticity

Essentalism
I prioritized my day according to what mattered most to me

Influence
I made a positive impact on others today

Urgency
I am aware that if I don't help people, they may never be helped.

Date __ / __ / __

Morning

Morning Mindset

The thing I am most excited about today is...

Something that might disrupt my success today is...

How I will deal with it...

A person who needs my help today is...

Someone I could surprise with an act of kindness today is...

Something I could do to demonstrate excellence or add true value to my community is...

One thing I could do to today that is out of my comfort zone is...

If I was a coach looking at my life, I would remind myself to remember that...

What is the one word I want to describe me as the best version of myself today?

I know today is a major success if...

Today's Top 3 Goals / Priorities

Morning Schedule		Point Value
5AM		
5:30		
6AM		
6:30		
7AM		
7:30		
8AM		
8:30		
9AM		
9:30		
10AM		
10:30		
11AM		

LIFE180

Daily Movement / Health

15 Point Day (Index of values for activities)

Make Appointment = 3 pts.
Have Meeting and schedule Follow Up = 3 pts.
Get Referral = 2 pts.
Application = 5 pts.
Policy Enforce = 5 pts.
Attend Network Event = 2pts.
Take Prospect/Client to Lunch/Event = 1 pt.
Send Affiliate Link to 5 People = 2 pts.
1 Hour of Reading or Education = 1 Pt.

Total Points

Afternoon

Tasks That Must be Completed

Who to connect with today

Afternoon Schedule

Point Value

12PM

12:30

1PM

1:30

2PM

2:30

3PM

3:30

4PM

4:30

5PM

5:30

6PM

Notes For Tomorrow / Appointments after 7PM

Daily Reflection

Something I truly appreciated about today was...

I am proud of the way I handled this task or situation today...

Something new I learned today was...
Today could have improved if I...

If I were my own coach, I would tell myself this about today...

Win The Day Scorecard

score yourself 1-5

Intention
I lived intentionally today according to my "why"

Energy
My physical and mental energy today

Boldness
Today I stepped out of my comfort zone in confidence and authenticity

Essentialism
I prioritized my day according to what mattered most to me

Influence
I made a positive impact on others today

Urgency
I am aware that if I don't help people, they may never be helped.

Date __ / __ / __

Morning

Morning Mindset

The thing I am most excited about today is...

Something that might disrupt my success today is...

How I will deal with it...

A person who needs my help today is...

Someone I could surprise with an act of kindness today is...

Something I could do to demonstrate excellence or add true value to my community is...

One thing I could do to today that is out of my comfort zone is...

If I was a coach looking at my life, I would remind myself to remember that...

What is the one word I want to describe me as the best version of myself today?

I know today is a major success if...

Today's Top 3 Goals / Priorities

Time	Morning Schedule	Point Value
5AM		
5:30		
6AM		
6:30		
7AM		
7:30		
8AM		
8:30		
9AM		
9:30		
10AM		
10:30		
11AM		

Daily Movement / Health

15 Point Day (Index of values for activities)

Make Appointment = 3 pts.
Have Meeting and schedule Follow Up = 3 pts.
Get Referral = 2 pts.
Application = 5 pts.
Policy Enforce = 5 pts.
Attend Network Event = 2pts.
Take Prospect/Client to Lunch/Event = 1 pt.
Send Affiliate Link to 5 People = 2 pts.
1 Hour of Reading or Education = 1 Pt.

Total Points

Afternoon

Tasks That Must be Completed

Who to connect with today

Afternoon Schedule

Point Value

12PM

12:30

1PM

1:30

2PM

2:30

3PM

3:30

4PM

4:30

5PM

5:30

6PM

Notes For Tomorrow / Appointments after 7PM

Daily Reflection

Something I truly appreciated about today was...

I am proud of the way I handled this task or situation today...

Something new I learned today was...
Today could have improved if I...

If I were my own coach, I would tell my-self this about today...

Win The Day Scorecard

score yourself 1-5

Intention
I lived intentionally today according to my "why"

Energy
My physical and mental energy today

Boldness
Today I stepped out of my comfort zone in confidence and authenticity

Essentialism
I prioritized my day according to what mattered most to me

Influence
I made a positive impact on others today

Urgency
I am aware that if I don't help people, they may never be helped.

Weekly Learning Review

Three or more amazing things that happened this week

The main struggle I had this past week was...

If you were coaching yourself, how would you coach yourself to handle this next week?

Two areas I grew in this week were...

Three things I learned about others this week (your loved ones, friends, clients, etc...)

Something I could have done to have more success in the areas that matter to me was...

Weekly Win The Day Review

At the end of every day this past week, you scored yourself according to INTENTION, ENERGY, URGENCY, ESSENTIALISM, INFLUENCE, & BOLDNESS. Add the scores up for each section and include them in the bubbles below. Don't be hard on yourself, but be honest. Take your number and divide by 2. The maximum score you can receive is 105.

Intention	Energy	Essentialism
Urgency	Influence	Boldness

Total	

Dates: _ _ / _ _ / _ _ - _ _ / _ _ / _ _

Weekly Business Reflection

The area I excelled most in this week and why...

Something I could have done this past week to achieve more success...

What I will do differently next week to elevate my performance...

What is the one activity I am not doing enough of?

Who on the team can help me elevate my performance through joint work or mentoring?

Who on the team can I serve or collaborate with in a mutually beneficial way?

What am I most proud of this week?

If you were your own coach, what would you tell yourself you need to do next week to achieve your results?

Weekly Business Point Tracking

Day	Total Points
Monday	
Tuesday	
Wednesday	
Thursday	
Friday	
Saturday	
Sunday	
Total	

Date __ / __ / __

Morning

Morning Mindset

The thing I am most excited about today is...

Something that might disrupt my success today is...

How I will deal with it...

A person who needs my help today is...

Someone I could surprise with an act of kindness today is...

Something I could do to demonstrate excellence or add true value to my community is...

One thing I could do to today that is out of my comfort zone is...

If I was a coach looking at my life, I would remind myself to remember that...

What is the one word I want to describe me as the best version of myself today?

I know today is a major success if...

Today's Top 3 Goals / Priorities

Morning Schedule		Point Value
5AM		
5:30		
6AM		
6:30		
7AM		
7:30		
8AM		
8:30		
9AM		
9:30		
10AM		
10:30		
11AM		

LIFE180

Daily Movement / Health

15 Point Day (Index of values for activities)

Make Appointment = 3 pts.
Have Meeting and schedule Follow Up = 3 pts.
Get Referral = 2 pts.
Application = 5 pts.
Policy Enforce = 5 pts.
Attend Network Event = 2pts.
Take Prospect/Client to Lunch/Event = 1 pt.
Send Affiliate Link to 5 People = 2 pts.
1 Hour of Reading or Education = 1 Pt.

Total Points

Afternoon

Tasks That Must be Completed

Who to connect with today

Afternoon Schedule | Point Value

12PM

12:30

1PM

1:30

2PM

2:30

3PM

3:30

4PM

4:30

5PM

5:30

6PM

Notes For Tomorrow / Appointments after 7PM

Daily Reflection

Something I truly appreciated about today was...

I am proud of the way I handled this task or situation today...

Something new I learned today was...

Today could have improved if I...

If I were my own coach, I would tell my-self this about today...

Win The Day Scorecard

score yourself 1-5

Intention
I lived intentionally today according to my "why"

Energy
My physical and mental energy today

Boldness
Today I stepped out of my comfort zone in confidence and authenticity

Essentalism
I prioritized my day according to what mattered most to me

Influence
I made a positive impact on others today

Urgency
I am aware that if I don't help people, they may never be helped.

Date __ / __ / __

Morning

Morning Mindset

The thing I am most excited about today is...

Something that might disrupt my success today is...

How I will deal with it...

A person who needs my help today is...

Someone I could surprise with an act of kindness today is...

Something I could do to demonstrate excellence or add true value to my community is...

One thing I could do to today that is out of my comfort zone is...

If I was a coach looking at my life, I would remind myself to remember that...

What is the one word I want to describe me as the best version of myself today?

I know today is a major success if...

Today's Top 3 Goals / Priorities

Morning Schedule		Point Value
5AM		
5:30		
6AM		
6:30		
7AM		
7:30		
8AM		
8:30		
9AM		
9:30		
10AM		
10:30		
11AM		

LIFE180

Daily Movement / Health

15 Point Day (Index of values for activities)

Make Appointment = 3 pts.
Have Meeting and schedule Follow Up = 3 pts.
Get Referral = 2 pts.
Application = 5 pts.
Policy Enforce = 5 pts.
Attend Network Event = 2pts.
Take Prospect/Client to Lunch/Event = 1 pt.
Send Affiliate Link to 5 People = 2 pts.
1 Hour of Reading or Education = 1 Pt.

Total Points

Afternoon

Tasks That Must be Completed

Who to connect with today

Afternoon Schedule

Point Value

12PM

12:30

1PM

1:30

2PM

2:30

3PM

3:30

4PM

4:30

5PM

5:30

6PM

Notes For Tomorrow / Appointments after 7PM

Daily Reflection

Something I truly appreciated about today was...

I am proud of the way I handled this task or situation today...

Something new I learned today was...
Today could have improved if I...

If I were my own coach, I would tell myself this about today...

Win The Day Scorecard

score yourself 1-5

Intention
I lived intentionally today according to my "why"

Energy
My physical and mental energy today

Boldness
Today I stepped out of my comfort zone in confidence and authenticity

Essentalism
I prioritized my day according to what mattered most to me

Influence
I made a positive impact on others today

Urgency
I am aware that if I don't help people, they may never be helped.

Date __ /__ / __

Morning

Morning Mindset

The thing I am most excited about today is...

Something that might disrupt my success today is...

How I will deal with it...

A person who needs my help today is...

Someone I could surprise with an act of kindness today is...

Something I could do to demonstrate excellence or add true value to my community is...

One thing I could do to today that is out of my comfort zone is...

If I was a coach looking at my life, I would remind myself to remember that...

What is the one word I want to describe me as the best version of myself today?

I know today is a major success if...

Today's Top 3 Goals / Priorities

Morning Schedule		Point Value
5AM		
5:30		
6AM		
6:30		
7AM		
7:30		
8AM		
8:30		
9AM		
9:30		
10AM		
10:30		
11AM		

LIFE180

Daily Movement / Health

15 Point Day (Index of values for activities)

Make Appointment = 3 pts.
Have Meeting and schedule Follow Up = 3 pts.
Get Referral = 2 pts.
Application = 5 pts.
Policy Enforce = 5 pts.
Attend Network Event = 2pts.
Take Prospect/Client to Lunch/Event = 1 pt.
Send Affiliate Link to 5 People = 2 pts.
1 Hour of Reading or Education = 1 Pt.

Total Points

Afternoon

Tasks That Must be Completed

Who to connect with today

Afternoon Schedule

Point Value

12PM

12:30

1PM

1:30

2PM

2:30

3PM

3:30

4PM

4:30

5PM

5:30

6PM

Notes For Tomorrow / Appointments after 7PM

Daily Reflection

Something I truly appreciated about today was...

I am proud of the way I handled this task or situation today...

Something new I learned today was...

Today could have improved if I...

If I were my own coach, I would tell myself this about today...

Win The Day Scorecard

score yourself 1-5

Intention
I lived intentionally today according to my "why"

Energy
My physical and mental energy today

Boldness
Today I stepped out of my comfort zone in confidence and authenticity

Essentalism
I prioritized my day according to what mattered most to me

Influence
I made a positive impact on others today

Urgency
I am aware that if I don't help people, they may never be helped.

Date __ /__ / __

Morning

Morning Mindset

The thing I am most excited about today is...

Something that might disrupt my success today is...

How I will deal with it...

A person who needs my help today is...

Someone I could surprise with an act of kindness today is...

Something I could do to demonstrate excellence or add true value to my community is...

One thing I could do to today that is out of my comfort zone is...

If I was a coach looking at my life, I would remind myself to remember that...

What is the one word I want to describe me as the best version of myself today?

I know today is a major success if...

Today's Top 3 Goals / Priorities

Morning Schedule		Point Value
5AM		
5:30		
6AM		
6:30		
7AM		
7:30		
8AM		
8:30		
9AM		
9:30		
10AM		
10:30		
11AM		

LIFE 180

Daily Movement / Health

15 Point Day (Index of values for activities)

Make Appointment = 3 pts.
Have Meeting and schedule Follow Up = 3 pts.
Get Referral = 2 pts.
Application = 5 pts.
Policy Enforce = 5 pts.
Attend Network Event = 2pts.
Take Prospect/Client to Lunch/Event = 1 pt.
Send Affiliate Link to 5 People = 2 pts.
1 Hour of Reading or Education = 1 Pt.

Total Points

Afternoon

Tasks That Must be Completed

Who to connect with today

Afternoon Schedule

Point Value

12PM

12:30

1PM

1:30

2PM

2:30

3PM

3:30

4PM

4:30

5PM

5:30

6PM

Notes For Tomorrow / Appointments after 7PM

Daily Reflection

Something I truly appreciated about today was...

I am proud of the way I handled this task or situation today...

Something new I learned today was...
Today could have improved if I...

If I were my own coach, I would tell myself this about today...

Win The Day Scorecard

score yourself 1-5

Intention
I lived intentionally today according to my "why"

Energy
My physical and mental energy today

Boldness
Today I stepped out of my comfort zone in confidence and authenticity

Essentialism
I prioritized my day according to what mattered most to me

Influence
I made a positive impact on others today

Urgency
I am aware that if I don't help people, they may never be helped.

Date __ / __ / __

Morning

Morning Mindset

The thing I am most excited about today is...

Something that might disrupt my success today is...

How I will deal with it...

A person who needs my help today is...

Someone I could surprise with an act of kindness today is...

Something I could do to demonstrate excellence or add true value to my community is...

One thing I could do to today that is out of my comfort zone is...

If I was a coach looking at my life, I would remind myself to remember that...

What is the one word I want to describe me as the best version of myself today?

I know today is a major success if...

Today's Top 3 Goals / Priorities

Morning Schedule		Point Value
5AM		
5:30		
6AM		
6:30		
7AM		
7:30		
8AM		
8:30		
9AM		
9:30		
10AM		
10:30		
11AM		

LIFE180

Daily Movement / Health

15 Point Day (Index of values for activities)

Make Appointment = 3 pts.
Have Meeting and schedule Follow Up = 3 pts.
Get Referral = 2 pts.
Application = 5 pts.
Policy Enforce = 5 pts.
Attend Network Event = 2pts.
Take Prospect/Client to Lunch/Event = 1 pt.
Send Affiliate Link to 5 People = 2 pts.
1 Hour of Reading or Education = 1 Pt.

Total Points

Afternoon

Tasks That Must be Completed

Who to connect with today

Afternoon Schedule

Point Value

12PM

12:30

1PM

1:30

2PM

2:30

3PM

3:30

4PM

4:30

5PM

5:30

6PM

Daily Reflection

Something I truly appreciated about today was...

I am proud of the way I handled this task or situation today...

Something new I learned today was...

Today could have improved if I...

If I were my own coach, I would tell my-self this about today...

Win The Day Scorecard

score yourself 1-5

Intention
I lived intentionally today according to my "why"

Energy
My physical and mental energy today

Boldness
Today I stepped out of my comfort zone in confidence and authenticity

Essentalism
I prioritized my day according to what mattered most to me

Influence
I made a positive impact on others today

Urgency
I am aware that if I don't help people, they may never be helped.

Notes For Tomorrow / Appointments after 7PM

Date __ / __ / __

Morning

Morning Mindset

The thing I am most excited about today is...

Something that might disrupt my success today is...

How I will deal with it...

A person who needs my help today is...

Someone I could surprise with an act of kindness today is...

Something I could do to demonstrate excellence or add true value to my community is...

One thing I could do to today that is out of my comfort zone is...

If I was a coach looking at my life, I would remind myself to remember that...

What is the one word I want to describe me as the best version of myself today?

I know today is a major success if...

Today's Top 3 Goals / Priorities

Morning Schedule		Point Value
5AM		
5:30		
6AM		
6:30		
7AM		
7:30		
8AM		
8:30		
9AM		
9:30		
10AM		
10:30		
11AM		

LIFE180

Daily Movement / Health

15 Point Day (Index of values for activities)

Make Appointment = 3 pts.
Have Meeting and schedule Follow Up = 3 pts.
Get Referral = 2 pts.
Application = 5 pts.
Policy Enforce = 5 pts.
Attend Network Event = 2pts.
Take Prospect/Client to Lunch/Event = 1 pt.
Send Affiliate Link to 5 People = 2 pts.
1 Hour of Reading or Education = 1 Pt.

Total Points

Afternoon

Tasks That Must be Completed

Who to connect with today

Afternoon Schedule

Point Value

12PM

12:30

1PM

1:30

2PM

2:30

3PM

3:30

4PM

4:30

5PM

5:30

6PM

Notes For Tomorrow / Appointments after 7PM

Daily Reflection

Something I truly appreciated about today was...

I am proud of the way I handled this task or situation today...

Something new I learned today was...

Today could have improved if I...

If I were my own coach, I would tell myself this about today...

Win The Day Scorecard

score yourself 1-5

Intention
I lived intentionally today according to my "why"

Energy
My physical and mental energy today

Boldness
Today I stepped out of my comfort zone in confidence and authenticity

Essentialism
I prioritized my day according to what mattered most to me

Influence
I made a positive impact on others today

Urgency
I am aware that if I don't help people, they may never be helped.

Date __ /__ / __

Morning

Morning Mindset

The thing I am most excited about today is...

Something that might disrupt my success today is...

How I will deal with it...

A person who needs my help today is...

Someone I could surprise with an act of kindness today is...

Something I could do to demonstrate excellence or add true value to my community is...

One thing I could do to today that is out of my comfort zone is...

If I was a coach looking at my life, I would remind myself to remember that...

What is the one word I want to describe me as the best version of myself today?

I know today is a major success if...

Today's Top 3 Goals / Priorities

Time	Morning Schedule	Point Value
5AM		
5:30		
6AM		
6:30		
7AM		
7:30		
8AM		
8:30		
9AM		
9:30		
10AM		
10:30		
11AM		

LIFE180

Daily Movement / Health

15 Point Day (Index of values for activities)

Make Appointment = 3 pts.
Have Meeting and schedule Follow Up = 3 pts.
Get Referral = 2 pts.
Application = 5 pts.
Policy Enforce = 5 pts.
Attend Network Event = 2pts.
Take Prospect/Client to Lunch/Event = 1 pt.
Send Affiliate Link to 5 People = 2 pts.
1 Hour of Reading or Education = 1 Pt.

Total Points

Afternoon

Tasks That Must be Completed

Who to connect with today

Afternoon Schedule

Point Value

12PM

12:30

1PM

1:30

2PM

2:30

3PM

3:30

4PM

4:30

5PM

5:30

6PM

Notes For Tomorrow / Appointments after 7PM

Daily Reflection

Something I truly appreciated about today was...

I am proud of the way I handled this task or situation today...

Something new I learned today was...

Today could have improved if I...

If I were my own coach, I would tell myself this about today...

Win The Day Scorecard

score yourself 1-5

Intention
I lived intentionally today according to my "why"

Energy
My physical and mental energy today

Boldness
Today I stepped out of my comfort zone in confidence and authenticity

Essentialism
I prioritized my day according to what mattered most to me

Influence
I made a positive impact on others today

Urgency
I am aware that if I don't help people, they may never be helped.

Weekly Learning Review

Three or more amazing things that happened this week

The main struggle I had this past week was...

If you were coaching yourself, how would you coach yourself to handle this next week?

Two areas I grew in this week were...

Three things I learned about others this week (your loved ones, friends, clients, etc...)

Something I could have done to have more success in the areas that matter to me was...

Weekly Win The Day Review

At the end of every day this past week, you scored yourself according to INTENTION, ENERGY, URGENCY, ESSENTIALISM, INFLUENCE, & BOLDNESS. Add the scores up for each section and include them in the bubbles below. Don't be hard on yourself, but be honest. Take your number and divide by 2. The maximum score you can receive is 105.

Intention	Energy	Essentialism
Urgency	**Influence**	**Boldness**

Dates: _ _ / _ _ / _ _ - _ _ / _ _ / _ _

Total	

Weekly Business Reflection

The area I excelled most in this week and why...

Something I could have done this past week to achieve more success...

What I will do differently next week to elevate my performance...

What is the one activity I am not doing enough of?

Who on the team can help me elevate my performance through joint work or mentoring?

Who on the team can I serve or collaborate with in a mutually beneficial way?

What am I most proud of this week?

If you were your own coach, what would you tell yourself you need to do next week to achieve your results?

Weekly Business Point Tracking

Day	Total Points
Monday	
Tuesday	
Wednesday	
Thursday	
Friday	
Saturday	
Sunday	
Total	

Date __ / __ / __

Morning

Morning Mindset

The thing I am most excited about today is...

Something that might disrupt my success today is...

How I will deal with it...

A person who needs my help today is...

Someone I could surprise with an act of kindness today is...

Something I could do to demonstrate excellence or add true value to my community is...

One thing I could do to today that is out of my comfort zone is...

If I was a coach looking at my life, I would remind myself to remember that...

What is the one word I want to describe me as the best version of myself today?

I know today is a major success if...

Today's Top 3 Goals / Priorities

Morning Schedule		Point Value
5AM		
5:30		
6AM		
6:30		
7AM		
7:30		
8AM		
8:30		
9AM		
9:30		
10AM		
10:30		
11AM		

LIFE180

Daily Movement / Health

15 Point Day (Index of values for activities)

Make Appointment = 3 pts.
Have Meeting and schedule Follow Up = 3 pts.
Get Referral = 2 pts.
Application = 5 pts.
Policy Enforce = 5 pts.
Attend Network Event = 2pts.
Take Prospect/Client to Lunch/Event = 1 pt.
Send Affiliate Link to 5 People = 2 pts.
1 Hour of Reading or Education = 1 Pt.

Total Points

Afternoon

Tasks That Must be Completed

Who to connect with today

Afternoon Schedule

Point Value

12PM

12:30

1PM

1:30

2PM

2:30

3PM

3:30

4PM

4:30

5PM

5:30

6PM

Notes For Tomorrow / Appointments after 7PM

Daily Reflection

Something I truly appreciated about today was...

I am proud of the way I handled this task or situation today...

Something new I learned today was...
Today could have improved if I...

If I were my own coach, I would tell my-self this about today...

Win The Day Scorecard

score yourself 1-5

Intention

I lived intentionally today according to my "why"

Energy

My physical and mental energy today

Boldness

Today I stepped out of my comfort zone in confidence and authenticity

Essentalism

I prioritized my day according to what mattered most to me

Influence

I made a positive impact on others today

Urgency

I am aware that if I don't help people, they may never be helped.

Date __ / __ / __

Morning

Morning Mindset

The thing I am most excited about today is...

Something that might disrupt my success today is...

How I will deal with it...

A person who needs my help today is...

Someone I could surprise with an act of kindness today is...

Something I could do to demonstrate excellence or add true value to my community is...

One thing I could do to today that is out of my comfort zone is...

If I was a coach looking at my life, I would remind myself to remember that...

What is the one word I want to describe me as the best version of myself today?

I know today is a major success if...

Today's Top 3 Goals / Priorities

Morning Schedule		Point Value
5AM		
5:30		
6AM		
6:30		
7AM		
7:30		
8AM		
8:30		
9AM		
9:30		
10AM		
10:30		
11AM		

Daily Movement / Health

15 Point Day (Index of values for activities)

Make Appointment = 3 pts.
Have Meeting and schedule Follow Up = 3 pts.
Get Referral = 2 pts.
Application = 5 pts.
Policy Enforce = 5 pts.
Attend Network Event = 2pts.
Take Prospect/Client to Lunch/Event = 1 pt.
Send Affiliate Link to 5 People = 2 pts.
1 Hour of Reading or Education = 1 Pt.

Total Points

Afternoon

Tasks That Must be Completed

Afternoon Schedule

Point Value

12PM

12:30

1PM

1:30

2PM

2:30

3PM

3:30

4PM

4:30

5PM

5:30

6PM

Notes For Tomorrow / Appointments after 7PM

Who to connect with today

Daily Reflection

Something I truly appreciated about today was...

I am proud of the way I handled this task or situation today...

Something new I learned today was...
Today could have improved if I...

If I were my own coach, I would tell myself this about today...

Win The Day Scorecard

score yourself 1-5

Intention
I lived intentionally today according to my "why"

Energy
My physical and mental energy today

Boldness
Today I stepped out of my comfort zone in confidence and authenticity

Essentialism
I prioritized my day according to what mattered most to me

Influence
I made a positive impact on others today

Urgency
I am aware that if I don't help people, they may never be helped.

Date __ / __ / __

Morning

Morning Mindset

The thing I am most excited about today is...

Something that might disrupt my success today is...

How I will deal with it...

A person who needs my help today is...

Someone I could surprise with an act of kindness today is...

Something I could do to demonstrate excellence or add true value to my community is...

One thing I could do to today that is out of my comfort zone is...

If I was a coach looking at my life, I would remind myself to remember that...

What is the one word I want to describe me as the best version of myself today?

I know today is a major success if...

Today's Top 3 Goals / Priorities

Morning Schedule		Point Value
5AM		
5:30		
6AM		
6:30		
7AM		
7:30		
8AM		
8:30		
9AM		
9:30		
10AM		
10:30		
11AM		

Daily Movement / Health

15 Point Day (Index of values for activities)

Make Appointment = 3 pts.
Have Meeting and schedule Follow Up = 3 pts.
Get Referral = 2 pts.
Application = 5 pts.
Policy Enforce = 5 pts.
Attend Network Event = 2pts.
Take Prospect/Client to Lunch/Event = 1 pt.
Send Affiliate Link to 5 People = 2 pts.
1 Hour of Reading or Education = 1 Pt.

Total Points

Afternoon

Tasks That Must be Completed

Afternoon Schedule | Point Value

12PM

12:30

1PM

1:30

2PM

2:30

3PM

3:30

4PM

4:30

5PM

5:30

6PM

Notes For Tomorrow / Appointments after 7PM

Who to connect with today

Daily Reflection

Something I truly appreciated about today was...

I am proud of the way I handled this task or situation today...

Something new I learned today was...
Today could have improved if I...

If I were my own coach, I would tell myself this about today...

Win The Day Scorecard

score yourself 1-5

Intention
I lived intentionally today according to my "why"

Energy
My physical and mental energy today

Boldness
Today I stepped out of my comfort zone in confidence and authenticity

Essentalism
I prioritized my day according to what mattered most to me

Influence
I made a positive impact on others today

Urgency
I am aware that if I don't help people, they may never be helped.

Date __ /__ / __

Morning

Morning Mindset

The thing I am most excited about today is...

Something that might disrupt my success today is...

How I will deal with it...

A person who needs my help today is...

Someone I could surprise with an act of kindness today is...

Something I could do to demonstrate excellence or add true value to my community is...

One thing I could do to today that is out of my comfort zone is...

If I was a coach looking at my life, I would remind myself to remember that...

What is the one word I want to describe me as the best version of myself today?

I know today is a major success if...

Today's Top 3 Goals / Priorities

Time	Morning Schedule	Point Value
5AM		
5:30		
6AM		
6:30		
7AM		
7:30		
8AM		
8:30		
9AM		
9:30		
10AM		
10:30		
11AM		

Daily Movement / Health

15 Point Day (Index of values for activities)

Make Appointment = 3 pts.
Have Meeting and schedule Follow Up = 3 pts.
Get Referral = 2 pts.
Application = 5 pts.
Policy Enforce = 5 pts.
Attend Network Event = 2pts.
Take Prospect/Client to Lunch/Event = 1 pt.
Send Affiliate Link to 5 People = 2 pts.
1 Hour of Reading or Education = 1 Pt.

Total Points

Afternoon

Tasks That Must be Completed

Who to connect with today

Afternoon Schedule

Point Value

12PM

12:30

1PM

1:30

2PM

2:30

3PM

3:30

4PM

4:30

5PM

5:30

6PM

Notes For Tomorrow / Appointments after 7PM

Daily Reflection

Something I truly appreciated about today was...

I am proud of the way I handled this task or situation today...

Something new I learned today was...

Today could have improved if I...

If I were my own coach, I would tell myself this about today...

Win The Day Scorecard

score yourself 1-5

Intention
I lived intentionally today according to my "why"

Energy
My physical and mental energy today

Boldness
Today I stepped out of my comfort zone in confidence and authenticity

Essentalism
I prioritized my day according to what mattered most to me

Influence
I made a positive impact on others today

Urgency
I am aware that if I don't help people, they may never be helped.

Date __ / __ / __

Morning

Morning Mindset

The thing I am most excited about today is...

Something that might disrupt my success today is...

How I will deal with it...

A person who needs my help today is...

Someone I could surprise with an act of kindness today is...

Something I could do to demonstrate excellence or add true value to my community is...

One thing I could do to today that is out of my comfort zone is...

If I was a coach looking at my life, I would remind myself to remember that...

What is the one word I want to describe me as the best version of myself today?

I know today is a major success if...

Today's Top 3 Goals / Priorities

Morning Schedule		Point Value
5AM		
5:30		
6AM		
6:30		
7AM		
7:30		
8AM		
8:30		
9AM		
9:30		
10AM		
10:30		
11AM		

LIFE180

Daily Movement / Health

15 Point Day (Index of values for activities)

Make Appointment = 3 pts.
Have Meeting and schedule Follow Up = 3 pts.
Get Referral = 2 pts.
Application = 5 pts.
Policy Enforce = 5 pts.
Attend Network Event = 2pts.
Take Prospect/Client to Lunch/Event = 1 pt.
Send Affiliate Link to 5 People = 2 pts.
1 Hour of Reading or Education = 1 Pt.

Total Points

Afternoon

Tasks That Must be Completed

Who to connect with today

Afternoon Schedule

Point Value

12PM

12:30

1PM

1:30

2PM

2:30

3PM

3:30

4PM

4:30

5PM

5:30

6PM

Notes For Tomorrow / Appointments after 7PM

Daily Reflection

Something I truly appreciated about today was...

I am proud of the way I handled this task or situation today...

Something new I learned today was...
Today could have improved if I...

If I were my own coach, I would tell myself this about today...

Win The Day Scorecard

score yourself 1-5

Intention
I lived intentionally today according to my "why"

Energy
My physical and mental energy today

Boldness
Today I stepped out of my comfort zone in confidence and authenticity

Essentialism
I prioritized my day according to what mattered most to me

Influence
I made a positive impact on others today

Urgency
I am aware that if I don't help people, they may never be helped.

Date __ / __ / __

Morning

Morning Mindset

The thing I am most excited about today is...

Something that might disrupt my success today is...

How I will deal with it...

A person who needs my help today is...

Someone I could surprise with an act of kindness today is...

Something I could do to demonstrate excellence or add true value to my community is...

One thing I could do to today that is out of my comfort zone is...

If I was a coach looking at my life, I would remind myself to remember that...

What is the one word I want to describe me as the best version of myself today?

I know today is a major success if...

Today's Top 3 Goals / Priorities

Morning Schedule		Point Value
5AM		
5:30		
6AM		
6:30		
7AM		
7:30		
8AM		
8:30		
9AM		
9:30		
10AM		
10:30		
11AM		

LIFE180

Daily Movement / Health

15 Point Day (Index of values for activities)

Make Appointment = 3 pts.
Have Meeting and schedule Follow Up = 3 pts.
Get Referral = 2 pts.
Application = 5 pts.
Policy Enforce = 5 pts.
Attend Network Event = 2pts.
Take Prospect/Client to Lunch/Event = 1 pt.
Send Affiliate Link to 5 People = 2 pts.
1 Hour of Reading or Education = 1 Pt.

Total Points

Afternoon

Tasks That Must be Completed

Who to connect with today

Afternoon Schedule

Point Value

12PM

12:30

1PM

1:30

2PM

2:30

3PM

3:30

4PM

4:30

5PM

5:30

6PM

Daily Reflection

Something I truly appreciated about today was...

I am proud of the way I handled this task or situation today...

Something new I learned today was...

Today could have improved if I...

If I were my own coach, I would tell myself this about today...

Notes For Tomorrow / Appointments after 7PM

Win The Day Scorecard

score yourself 1-5

Intention
I lived intentionally today according to my "why"

Energy
My physical and mental energy today

Boldness
Today I stepped out of my comfort zone in confidence and authenticity

Essentialism
I prioritized my day according to what mattered most to me

Influence
I made a positive impact on others today

Urgency
I am aware that if I don't help people, they may never be helped.

Date __ / __ / __

Morning

Morning Mindset

The thing I am most excited about today is...

Something that might disrupt my success today is...

How I will deal with it...

A person who needs my help today is...

Someone I could surprise with an act of kindness today is...

Something I could do to demonstrate excellence or add true value to my community is...

One thing I could do to today that is out of my comfort zone is...

If I was a coach looking at my life, I would remind myself to remember that...

What is the one word I want to describe me as the best version of myself today?

I know today is a major success if...

Today's Top 3 Goals / Priorities

Morning Schedule		Point Value
5AM		
5:30		
6AM		
6:30		
7AM		
7:30		
8AM		
8:30		
9AM		
9:30		
10AM		
10:30		
11AM		

Daily Movement / Health

15 Point Day (Index of values for activities)

Make Appointment = 3 pts.
Have Meeting and schedule Follow Up = 3 pts.
Get Referral = 2 pts.
Application = 5 pts.
Policy Enforce = 5 pts.
Attend Network Event = 2pts.
Take Prospect/Client to Lunch/Event = 1 pt.
Send Affiliate Link to 5 People = 2 pts.
1 Hour of Reading or Education = 1 Pt.

Total Points

Afternoon

Tasks That Must be Completed

Who to connect with today

Afternoon Schedule | Point Value

12PM

12:30

1PM

1:30

2PM

2:30

3PM

3:30

4PM

4:30

5PM

5:30

6PM

Notes For Tomorrow / Appointments after 7PM

Daily Reflection

Something I truly appreciated about today was...

I am proud of the way I handled this task or situation today...

Something new I learned today was...
Today could have improved if I...

If I were my own coach, I would tell myself this about today...

Win The Day Scorecard

score yourself 1-5

Intention
I lived intentionally today according to my "why"

Energy
My physical and mental energy today

Boldness
Today I stepped out of my comfort zone in confidence and authenticity

Essentialism
I prioritized my day according to what mattered most to me

Influence
I made a positive impact on others today

Urgency
I am aware that if I don't help people, they may never be helped.

Weekly Learning Review

Three or more amazing things that happened this week

The main struggle I had this past week was...

If you were coaching yourself, how would you coach yourself to handle this next week?

Two areas I grew in this week were...

Three things I learned about others this week (your loved ones, friends, clients, etc...)

Something I could have done to have more success in the areas that matter to me was...

Weekly Win The Day Review

At the end of every day this past week, you scored yourself according to INTENTION, ENERGY, URGENCY, ESSENTIALISM, INFLUENCE, & BOLDNESS. Add the scores up for each section and include them in the bubbles below. Don't be hard on yourself, but be honest. Take your number and divide by 2. The maximum score you can receive is 105.

Intention	Energy	Essentialism
Urgency	Influence	Boldness

Dates: _ _ / _ _ / _ _ - _ _ / _ _ / _ _

Total	

Weekly Business Reflection

The area I excelled most in this week and why...

Something I could have done this past week to achieve more success...

What I will do differently next week to elevate my performance...

What is the one activity I am not doing enough of?

Who on the team can help me elevate my performance through joint work or mentoring?

Who on the team can I serve or collaborate with in a mutually beneficial way?

What am I most proud of this week?

If you were your own coach, what would you tell yourself you need to do next week to achieve your results?

Weekly Business Point Tracking

Day	Total Points
Monday	
Tuesday	
Wednesday	
Thursday	
Friday	
Saturday	
Sunday	
Total	

Date __ / __ / __

Morning

Morning Mindset

The thing I am most excited about today is...

Something that might disrupt my success today is...

How I will deal with it...

A person who needs my help today is...

Someone I could surprise with an act of kindness today is...

Something I could do to demonstrate excellence or add true value to my community is...

One thing I could do to today that is out of my comfort zone is...

If I was a coach looking at my life, I would remind myself to remember that...

What is the one word I want to describe me as the best version of myself today?

I know today is a major success if...

Today's Top 3 Goals / Priorities

Morning Schedule		Point Value
5AM		
5:30		
6AM		
6:30		
7AM		
7:30		
8AM		
8:30		
9AM		
9:30		
10AM		
10:30		
11AM		

LIFE180

Daily Movement / Health

15 Point Day (Index of values for activities)

Make Appointment = 3 pts.
Have Meeting and schedule Follow Up = 3 pts.
Get Referral = 2 pts.
Application = 5 pts.
Policy Enforce = 5 pts.
Attend Network Event = 2pts.
Take Prospect/Client to Lunch/Event = 1 pt.
Send Affiliate Link to 5 People = 2 pts.
1 Hour of Reading or Education = 1 Pt.

Total Points

Afternoon

Tasks That Must be Completed

Who to connect with today

Afternoon Schedule

Point Value

12PM

12:30

1PM

1:30

2PM

2:30

3PM

3:30

4PM

4:30

5PM

5:30

6PM

Notes For Tomorrow / Appointments after 7PM

Daily Reflection

Something I truly appreciated about today was...

I am proud of the way I handled this task or situation today...

Something new I learned today was...
Today could have improved if I...

If I were my own coach, I would tell my-self this about today...

Win The Day Scorecard

score yourself 1-5

Intention
I lived intentionally today according to my "why"

Energy
My physical and mental energy today

Boldness
Today I stepped out of my comfort zone in confidence and authenticity

Essentalism
I prioritized my day according to what mattered most to me

Influence
I made a positive impact on others today

Urgency
I am aware that if I don't help people, they may never be helped.

Date __ / __ / __

Morning

Morning Mindset

The thing I am most excited about today is...

Something that might disrupt my success today is...

How I will deal with it...

A person who needs my help today is...

Someone I could surprise with an act of kindness today is...

Something I could do to demonstrate excellence or add true value to my community is...

One thing I could do to today that is out of my comfort zone is...

If I was a coach looking at my life, I would remind myself to remember that...

What is the one word I want to describe me as the best version of myself today?

I know today is a major success if...

Today's Top 3 Goals / Priorities

Time	Morning Schedule	Point Value
5AM		
5:30		
6AM		
6:30		
7AM		
7:30		
8AM		
8:30		
9AM		
9:30		
10AM		
10:30		
11AM		

LIFE180

Daily Movement / Health

15 Point Day (Index of values for activities)

Make Appointment = 3 pts.
Have Meeting and schedule Follow Up = 3 pts.
Get Referral = 2 pts.
Application = 5 pts.
Policy Enforce = 5 pts.
Attend Network Event = 2pts.
Take Prospect/Client to Lunch/Event = 1 pt.
Send Affiliate Link to 5 People = 2 pts.
1 Hour of Reading or Education = 1 Pt.

Total Points

Afternoon

Tasks That Must be Completed

Who to connect with today

Afternoon Schedule

Point Value

12PM

12:30

1PM

1:30

2PM

2:30

3PM

3:30

4PM

4:30

5PM

5:30

6PM

Notes For Tomorrow / Appointments after 7PM

Daily Reflection

Something I truly appreciated about today was...

I am proud of the way I handled this task or situation today...

Something new I learned today was...
Today could have improved if I...

If I were my own coach, I would tell myself this about today...

Win The Day Scorecard

score yourself 1-5

Intention
I lived intentionally today according to my "why"

Energy
My physical and mental energy today

Boldness
Today I stepped out of my comfort zone in confidence and authenticity

Essentialism
I prioritized my day according to what mattered most to me

Influence
I made a positive impact on others today

Urgency
I am aware that if I don't help people, they may never be helped.

Date __ /__ / __

Morning

Morning Mindset

The thing I am most excited about today is...

Something that might disrupt my success today is...

How I will deal with it...

A person who needs my help today is...

Someone I could surprise with an act of kindness today is...

Something I could do to demonstrate excellence or add true value to my community is...

One thing I could do to today that is out of my comfort zone is...

If I was a coach looking at my life, I would remind myself to remember that...

What is the one word I want to describe me as the best version of myself today?

I know today is a major success if...

Today's Top 3 Goals / Priorities

Morning Schedule		Point Value
5AM		
5:30		
6AM		
6:30		
7AM		
7:30		
8AM		
8:30		
9AM		
9:30		
10AM		
10:30		
11AM		

Daily Movement / Health

15 Point Day (Index of values for activities)

Make Appointment = 3 pts.
Have Meeting and schedule Follow Up = 3 pts.
Get Referral = 2 pts.
Application = 5 pts.
Policy Enforce = 5 pts.
Attend Network Event = 2pts.
Take Prospect/Client to Lunch/Event = 1 pt.
Send Affiliate Link to 5 People = 2 pts.
1 Hour of Reading or Education = 1 Pt.

Total Points

Afternoon

Tasks That Must be Completed

Who to connect with today

Afternoon Schedule

Point Value

12PM

12:30

1PM

1:30

2PM

2:30

3PM

3:30

4PM

4:30

5PM

5:30

6PM

Notes For Tomorrow / Appointments after 7PM

Daily Reflection

Something I truly appreciated about today was...

I am proud of the way I handled this task or situation today...

Something new I learned today was...
Today could have improved if I...

If I were my own coach, I would tell my-self this about today...

Win The Day Scorecard

score yourself 1-5

Intention
I lived intentionally today according to my "why"

Energy
My physical and mental energy today

Boldness
Today I stepped out of my comfort zone in confidence and authenticity

Essentialism
I prioritized my day according to what mattered most to me

Influence
I made a positive impact on others today

Urgency
I am aware that if I don't help people, they may never be helped.

Date __ / __ / __

Morning

Morning Mindset

The thing I am most excited about today is...

Something that might disrupt my success today is...

How I will deal with it...

A person who needs my help today is...

Someone I could surprise with an act of kindness today is...

Something I could do to demonstrate excellence or add true value to my community is...

One thing I could do to today that is out of my comfort zone is...

If I was a coach looking at my life, I would remind myself to remember that...

What is the one word I want to describe me as the best version of myself today?

I know today is a major success if...

Today's Top 3 Goals / Priorities

Morning Schedule		Point Value
5AM		
5:30		
6AM		
6:30		
7AM		
7:30		
8AM		
8:30		
9AM		
9:30		
10AM		
10:30		
11AM		

LIFE180

Daily Movement / Health

15 Point Day (Index of values for activities)

Make Appointment = 3 pts.
Have Meeting and schedule Follow Up = 3 pts.
Get Referral = 2 pts.
Application = 5 pts.
Policy Enforce = 5 pts.
Attend Network Event = 2pts.
Take Prospect/Client to Lunch/Event = 1 pt.
Send Affiliate Link to 5 People = 2 pts.
1 Hour of Reading or Education = 1 Pt.

Total Points

Afternoon

Tasks That Must be Completed

Who to connect with today

Afternoon Schedule

Point Value

12PM

12:30

1PM

1:30

2PM

2:30

3PM

3:30

4PM

4:30

5PM

5:30

6PM

Notes For Tomorrow / Appointments after 7PM

Daily Reflection

Something I truly appreciated about today was...

I am proud of the way I handled this task or situation today...

Something new I learned today was...

Today could have improved if I...

If I were my own coach, I would tell myself this about today...

Win The Day Scorecard

score yourself 1-5

Intention
I lived intentionally today according to my "why"

Energy
My physical and mental energy today

Boldness
Today I stepped out of my comfort zone in confidence and authenticity

Essentalism
I prioritized my day according to what mattered most to me

Influence
I made a positive impact on others today

Urgency
I am aware that if I don't help people, they may never be helped.

Date __ / __ / __

Morning

Morning Mindset

The thing I am most excited about today is...

Something that might disrupt my success today is...

How I will deal with it...

A person who needs my help today is...

Someone I could surprise with an act of kindness today is...

Something I could do to demonstrate excellence or add true value to my community is...

One thing I could do to today that is out of my comfort zone is...

If I was a coach looking at my life, I would remind myself to remember that...

What is the one word I want to describe me as the best version of myself today?

I know today is a major success if...

Today's Top 3 Goals / Priorities

Morning Schedule		Point Value
5AM		
5:30		
6AM		
6:30		
7AM		
7:30		
8AM		
8:30		
9AM		
9:30		
10AM		
10:30		
11AM		

LIFE180

Daily Movement / Health

15 Point Day (Index of values for activities)

Make Appointment = 3 pts.
Have Meeting and schedule Follow Up = 3 pts.
Get Referral = 2 pts.
Application = 5 pts.
Policy Enforce = 5 pts.
Attend Network Event = 2pts.
Take Prospect/Client to Lunch/Event = 1 pt.
Send Affiliate Link to 5 People = 2 pts.
1 Hour of Reading or Education = 1 Pt.

Total Points

Afternoon

Tasks That Must be Completed

Who to connect with today

Afternoon Schedule

Point Value

12PM

12:30

1PM

1:30

2PM

2:30

3PM

3:30

4PM

4:30

5PM

5:30

6PM

Daily Reflection

Something I truly appreciated about today was...

I am proud of the way I handled this task or situation today...

Something new I learned today was...

Today could have improved if I...

If I were my own coach, I would tell myself this about today...

Win The Day Scorecard

score yourself 1-5

Intention
I lived intentionally today according to my "why"

Energy
My physical and mental energy today

Boldness
Today I stepped out of my comfort zone in confidence and authenticity

Essentialism
I prioritized my day according to what mattered most to me

Influence
I made a positive impact on others today

Urgency
I am aware that if I don't help people, they may never be helped.

Notes For Tomorrow / Appointments after 7PM

Date __ /__ / __

Morning

Morning Mindset

The thing I am most excited about today is...

Something that might disrupt my success today is...

How I will deal with it...

A person who needs my help today is...

Someone I could surprise with an act of kindness today is...

Something I could do to demonstrate excellence or add true value to my community is...

One thing I could do to today that is out of my comfort zone is...

If I was a coach looking at my life, I would remind myself to remember that...

What is the one word I want to describe me as the best version of myself today?

I know today is a major success if...

Today's Top 3 Goals / Priorities

Morning Schedule		Point Value
5AM		
5:30		
6AM		
6:30		
7AM		
7:30		
8AM		
8:30		
9AM		
9:30		
10AM		
10:30		
11AM		

Daily Movement / Health

15 Point Day (Index of values for activities)

Make Appointment = 3 pts.
Have Meeting and schedule Follow Up = 3 pts.
Get Referral = 2 pts.
Application = 5 pts.
Policy Enforce = 5 pts.
Attend Network Event = 2pts.
Take Prospect/Client to Lunch/Event = 1 pt.
Send Affiliate Link to 5 People = 2 pts.
1 Hour of Reading or Education = 1 Pt.

Total Points

Afternoon

Tasks That Must be Completed

Afternoon Schedule

Point Value

12PM

12:30

1PM

1:30

2PM

2:30

3PM

3:30

4PM

4:30

5PM

5:30

6PM

Notes For Tomorrow / Appointments after 7PM

LIFE 180

Who to connect with today

Daily Reflection

Something I truly appreciated about today was...

I am proud of the way I handled this task or situation today...

Something new I learned today was...
Today could have improved if I...

If I were my own coach, I would tell myself this about today...

Win The Day Scorecard

score yourself 1-5

Intention
I lived intentionally today according to my "why"

Energy
My physical and mental energy today

Boldness
Today I stepped out of my comfort zone in confidence and authenticity

Essentialism
I prioritized my day according to what mattered most to me

Influence
I made a positive impact on others today

Urgency
I am aware that if I don't help people, they may never be helped.

Date __ /__ / __

Morning

Morning Mindset

The thing I am most excited about today is...

Something that might disrupt my success today is...

How I will deal with it...

A person who needs my help today is...

Someone I could surprise with an act of kindness today is...

Something I could do to demonstrate excellence or add true value to my community is...

One thing I could do to today that is out of my comfort zone is...

If I was a coach looking at my life, I would remind myself to remember that...

What is the one word I want to describe me as the best version of myself today?

I know today is a major success if...

Today's Top 3 Goals / Priorities

Morning Schedule		Point Value
5AM		
5:30		
6AM		
6:30		
7AM		
7:30		
8AM		
8:30		
9AM		
9:30		
10AM		
10:30		
11AM		

Daily Movement / Health

15 Point Day (Index of values for activities)

Make Appointment = 3 pts.
Have Meeting and schedule Follow Up = 3 pts.
Get Referral = 2 pts.
Application = 5 pts.
Policy Enforce = 5 pts.
Attend Network Event = 2pts.
Take Prospect/Client to Lunch/Event = 1 pt.
Send Affiliate Link to 5 People = 2 pts.
1 Hour of Reading or Education = 1 Pt.

Total Points

Afternoon

Tasks That Must be Completed

Who to connect with today

Afternoon Schedule

Point Value

12PM

12:30

1PM

1:30

2PM

2:30

3PM

3:30

4PM

4:30

5PM

5:30

6PM

Notes For Tomorrow / Appointments after 7PM

Daily Reflection

Something I truly appreciated about today was...

I am proud of the way I handled this task or situation today...

Something new I learned today was...
Today could have improved if I...

If I were my own coach, I would tell myself this about today...

Win The Day Scorecard

score yourself 1-5

Intention
I lived intentionally today according to my "why"

Energy
My physical and mental energy today

Boldness
Today I stepped out of my comfort zone in confidence and authenticity

Essentialism
I prioritized my day according to what mattered most to me

Influence
I made a positive impact on others today

Urgency
I am aware that if I don't help people, they may never be helped.

Weekly Learning Review

Three or more amazing things that happened this week

The main struggle I had this past week was...

If you were coaching yourself, how would you coach yourself to handle this next week?

Two areas I grew in this week were...

Three things I learned about others this week (your loved ones, friends, clients, etc...)

Something I could have done to have more success in the areas that matter to me was...

Weekly Win The Day Review

At the end of every day this past week, you scored yourself according to INTENTION, ENERGY, URGENCY, ESSENTIALISM, INFLUENCE, & BOLDNESS. Add the scores up for each section and include them in the bubbles below. Don't be hard on yourself, but be honest. Take your number and divide by 2. The maximum score you can receive is 105.

Intention	Energy	Essentialism
Urgency	**Influence**	**Boldness**

Dates: _ _ / _ _ / _ _ - _ _ / _ _ / _ _

Total

Weekly Business Reflection

The area I excelled most in this week and why...

Something I could have done this past week to achieve more success...

What I will do differently next week to elevate my performance...

What is the one activity I am not doing enough of?

Who on the team can help me elevate my performance through joint work or mentoring?

Who on the team can I serve or collaborate with in a mutually beneficial way?

What am I most proud of this week?

If you were your own coach, what would you tell yourself you need to do next week to achieve your results?

Weekly Business Point Tracking

Day	Total Points
Monday	
Tuesday	
Wednesday	
Thursday	
Friday	
Saturday	
Sunday	
Total	

Date __ / __ / __

Morning

Morning Mindset

The thing I am most excited about today is...

Something that might disrupt my success today is...

How I will deal with it...

A person who needs my help today is...

Someone I could surprise with an act of kindness today is...

Something I could do to demonstrate excellence or add true value to my community is...

One thing I could do to today that is out of my comfort zone is...

If I was a coach looking at my life, I would remind myself to remember that...

What is the one word I want to describe me as the best version of myself today?

I know today is a major success if...

Today's Top 3 Goals / Priorities

Time	Morning Schedule	Point Value
5AM		
5:30		
6AM		
6:30		
7AM		
7:30		
8AM		
8:30		
9AM		
9:30		
10AM		
10:30		
11AM		

Daily Movement / Health

15 Point Day (Index of values for activities)

Make Appointment = 3 pts.
Have Meeting and schedule Follow Up = 3 pts.
Get Referral = 2 pts.
Application = 5 pts.
Policy Enforce = 5 pts.
Attend Network Event = 2pts.
Take Prospect/Client to Lunch/Event = 1 pt.
Send Affiliate Link to 5 People = 2 pts.
1 Hour of Reading or Education = 1 Pt.

Total Points

Afternoon

Tasks That Must be Completed

Who to connect with today

Afternoon Schedule

Point Value

12PM

12:30

1PM

1:30

2PM

2:30

3PM

3:30

4PM

4:30

5PM

5:30

6PM

Daily Reflection

Something I truly appreciated about today was...

I am proud of the way I handled this task or situation today...

Something new I learned today was...
Today could have improved if I...

If I were my own coach, I would tell myself this about today...

Win The Day Scorecard

score yourself 1-5

Intention
I lived intentionally today according to my "why"

Energy
My physical and mental energy today

Boldness
Today I stepped out of my comfort zone in confidence and authenticity

Essentialism
I prioritized my day according to what mattered most to me

Influence
I made a positive impact on others today

Urgency
I am aware that if I don't help people, they may never be helped.

Notes For Tomorrow / Appointments after 7PM

Date __ / __ / __

Morning

Morning Mindset

The thing I am most excited about today is...

Something that might disrupt my success today is...

How I will deal with it...

A person who needs my help today is...

Someone I could surprise with an act of kindness today is...

Something I could do to demonstrate excellence or add true value to my community is...

One thing I could do to today that is out of my comfort zone is...

If I was a coach looking at my life, I would remind myself to remember that...

What is the one word I want to describe me as the best version of myself today?

I know today is a major success if...

Today's Top 3 Goals / Priorities

Morning Schedule		Point Value
5AM		
5:30		
6AM		
6:30		
7AM		
7:30		
8AM		
8:30		
9AM		
9:30		
10AM		
10:30		
11AM		

Daily Movement / Health

15 Point Day (Index of values for activities)

Make Appointment = 3 pts.
Have Meeting and schedule Follow Up = 3 pts.
Get Referral = 2 pts.
Application = 5 pts.
Policy Enforce = 5 pts.
Attend Network Event = 2pts.
Take Prospect/Client to Lunch/Event = 1 pt.
Send Affiliate Link to 5 People = 2 pts.
1 Hour of Reading or Education = 1 Pt.

Total Points

Afternoon

Tasks That Must be Completed

Afternoon Schedule

Point Value

12PM

12:30

1PM

1:30

2PM

2:30

3PM

3:30

4PM

4:30

5PM

5:30

6PM

Notes For Tomorrow / Appointments after 7PM

Who to connect with today

Daily Reflection

Something I truly appreciated about today was...

I am proud of the way I handled this task or situation today...

Something new I learned today was...
Today could have improved if I...

If I were my own coach, I would tell my-self this about today...

Win The Day Scorecard

score yourself 1-5

Intention
I lived intentionally today according to my "why"

Energy
My physical and mental energy today

Boldness
Today I stepped out of my comfort zone in confidence and authenticity

Essentialism
I prioritized my day according to what mattered most to me

Influence
I made a positive impact on others today

Urgency
I am aware that if I don't help people, they may never be helped.

Date __ /__ / __

Morning

Morning Mindset

The thing I am most excited about today is...

Something that might disrupt my success today is...

How I will deal with it...

A person who needs my help today is...

Someone I could surprise with an act of kindness today is...

Something I could do to demonstrate excellence or add true value to my community is...

One thing I could do to today that is out of my comfort zone is...

If I was a coach looking at my life, I would remind myself to remember that...

What is the one word I want to describe me as the best version of myself today?

I know today is a major success if...

Today's Top 3 Goals / Priorities

Morning Schedule		Point Value
5AM		
5:30		
6AM		
6:30		
7AM		
7:30		
8AM		
8:30		
9AM		
9:30		
10AM		
10:30		
11AM		

Daily Movement / Health

15 Point Day (Index of values for activities)

Make Appointment = 3 pts.
Have Meeting and schedule Follow Up = 3 pts.
Get Referral = 2 pts.
Application = 5 pts.
Policy Enforce = 5 pts.
Attend Network Event = 2pts.
Take Prospect/Client to Lunch/Event = 1 pt.
Send Affiliate Link to 5 People = 2 pts.
1 Hour of Reading or Education = 1 Pt.

Total Points

Afternoon

Tasks That Must be Completed

Who to connect with today

Afternoon Schedule	Point Value
12PM	
12:30	
1PM	
1:30	
2PM	
2:30	
3PM	
3:30	
4PM	
4:30	
5PM	
5:30	
6PM	

Notes For Tomorrow / Appointments after 7PM

Daily Reflection

Something I truly appreciated about today was...

I am proud of the way I handled this task or situation today...

Something new I learned today was...

Today could have improved if I...

If I were my own coach, I would tell myself this about today...

Win The Day Scorecard

score yourself 1-5

Intention
I lived intentionally today according to my "why"

Energy
My physical and mental energy today

Boldness
Today I stepped out of my comfort zone in confidence and authenticity

Essentialism
I prioritized my day according to what mattered most to me

Influence
I made a positive impact on others today

Urgency
I am aware that if I don't help people, they may never be helped.

Date __ /__ / __

Morning

Morning Mindset

The thing I am most excited about today is...

Something that might disrupt my success today is...

How I will deal with it...

A person who needs my help today is...

Someone I could surprise with an act of kindness today is...

Something I could do to demonstrate excellence or add true value to my community is...

One thing I could do to today that is out of my comfort zone is...

If I was a coach looking at my life, I would remind myself to remember that...

What is the one word I want to describe me as the best version of myself today?

I know today is a major success if...

Today's Top 3 Goals / Priorities

Morning Schedule		Point Value
5AM		
5:30		
6AM		
6:30		
7AM		
7:30		
8AM		
8:30		
9AM		
9:30		
10AM		
10:30		
11AM		

Daily Movement / Health

15 Point Day (Index of values for activities)

Make Appointment = 3 pts.
Have Meeting and schedule Follow Up = 3 pts.
Get Referral = 2 pts.
Application = 5 pts.
Policy Enforce = 5 pts.
Attend Network Event = 2pts.
Take Prospect/Client to Lunch/Event = 1 pt.
Send Affiliate Link to 5 People = 2 pts.
1 Hour of Reading or Education = 1 Pt.

Total Points

Afternoon

Tasks That Must be Completed

Who to connect with today

Afternoon Schedule

Point Value

12PM

12:30

1PM

1:30

2PM

2:30

3PM

3:30

4PM

4:30

5PM

5:30

6PM

Daily Reflection

Something I truly appreciated about today was...

I am proud of the way I handled this task or situation today...

Something new I learned today was...

Today could have improved if I...

If I were my own coach, I would tell myself this about today...

Notes For Tomorrow / Appointments after 7PM

LIFE180

Win The Day Scorecard

score yourself 1-5

Intention
I lived intentionally today according to my "why"

Energy
My physical and mental energy today

Boldness
Today I stepped out of my comfort zone in confidence and authenticity

Essentialism
I prioritized my day according to what mattered most to me

Influence
I made a positive impact on others today

Urgency
I am aware that if I don't help people, they may never be helped.

Date __ /__ / __

Morning

Morning Mindset

The thing I am most excited about today is...

Something that might disrupt my success today is...

How I will deal with it...

A person who needs my help today is...

Someone I could surprise with an act of kindness today is...

Something I could do to demonstrate excellence or add true value to my community is...

One thing I could do to today that is out of my comfort zone is...

If I was a coach looking at my life, I would remind myself to remember that...

What is the one word I want to describe me as the best version of myself today?

I know today is a major success if...

Today's Top 3 Goals / Priorities

Morning Schedule		Point Value
5AM		
5:30		
6AM		
6:30		
7AM		
7:30		
8AM		
8:30		
9AM		
9:30		
10AM		
10:30		
11AM		

Daily Movement / Health

15 Point Day (Index of values for activities)

Make Appointment = 3 pts.
Have Meeting and schedule Follow Up = 3 pts.
Get Referral = 2 pts.
Application = 5 pts.
Policy Enforce = 5 pts.
Attend Network Event = 2pts.
Take Prospect/Client to Lunch/Event = 1 pt.
Send Affiliate Link to 5 People = 2 pts.
1 Hour of Reading or Education = 1 Pt.

Total Points

Afternoon

Tasks That Must be Completed

Who to connect with today

Afternoon Schedule

Point Value

12PM

12:30

1PM

1:30

2PM

2:30

3PM

3:30

4PM

4:30

5PM

5:30

6PM

Notes For Tomorrow / Appointments after 7PM

Daily Reflection

Something I truly appreciated about today was...

I am proud of the way I handled this task or situation today...

Something new I learned today was...

Today could have improved if I...

If I were my own coach, I would tell my-self this about today...

Win The Day Scorecard

score yourself 1-5

Intention
I lived intentionally today according to my "why"

Energy
My physical and mental energy today

Boldness
Today I stepped out of my comfort zone in confidence and authenticity

Essentialism
I prioritized my day according to what mattered most to me

Influence
I made a positive impact on others today

Urgency
I am aware that if I don't help people, they may never be helped.

Date __ / __ / __

Morning

Morning Mindset

The thing I am most excited about today is...

Something that might disrupt my success today is...

How I will deal with it...

A person who needs my help today is...

Someone I could surprise with an act of kindness today is...

Something I could do to demonstrate excellence or add true value to my community is...

One thing I could do to today that is out of my comfort zone is...

If I was a coach looking at my life, I would remind myself to remember that...

What is the one word I want to describe me as the best version of myself today?

I know today is a major success if...

Today's Top 3 Goals / Priorities

Morning Schedule

	Morning Schedule	Point Value
5AM		
5:30		
6AM		
6:30		
7AM		
7:30		
8AM		
8:30		
9AM		
9:30		
10AM		
10:30		
11AM		

Daily Movement / Health

15 Point Day (Index of values for activities)

Make Appointment = 3 pts.
Have Meeting and schedule Follow Up = 3 pts.
Get Referral = 2 pts.
Application = 5 pts.
Policy Enforce = 5 pts.
Attend Network Event = 2pts.
Take Prospect/Client to Lunch/Event = 1 pt.
Send Affiliate Link to 5 People = 2 pts.
1 Hour of Reading or Education = 1 Pt.

Total Points

Afternoon

Tasks That Must be Completed

Who to connect with today

Afternoon Schedule

Point Value

12PM

12:30

1PM

1:30

2PM

2:30

3PM

3:30

4PM

4:30

5PM

5:30

6PM

Notes For Tomorrow / Appointments after 7PM

Daily Reflection

Something I truly appreciated about today was...

I am proud of the way I handled this task or situation today...

Something new I learned today was...

Today could have improved if I...

If I were my own coach, I would tell my-self this about today...

Win The Day Scorecard

score yourself 1-5

Intention
I lived intentionally today according to my "why"

Energy
My physical and mental energy today

Boldness
Today I stepped out of my comfort zone in confidence and authenticity

Essentialism
I prioritized my day according to what mattered most to me

Influence
I made a positive impact on others today

Urgency
I am aware that if I don't help people, they may never be helped.

Date __ / __ / __

Morning

Morning Mindset

The thing I am most excited about today is...

Something that might disrupt my success today is...

How I will deal with it...

A person who needs my help today is...

Someone I could surprise with an act of kindness today is...

Something I could do to demonstrate excellence or add true value to my community is...

One thing I could do to today that is out of my comfort zone is...

If I was a coach looking at my life, I would remind myself to remember that...

What is the one word I want to describe me as the best version of myself today?

I know today is a major success if...

Today's Top 3 Goals / Priorities

Time	Morning Schedule	Point Value
5AM		
5:30		
6AM		
6:30		
7AM		
7:30		
8AM		
8:30		
9AM		
9:30		
10AM		
10:30		
11AM		

Daily Movement / Health

15 Point Day (Index of values for activities)

Make Appointment = 3 pts.
Have Meeting and schedule Follow Up = 3 pts.
Get Referral = 2 pts.
Application = 5 pts.
Policy Enforce = 5 pts.
Attend Network Event = 2pts.
Take Prospect/Client to Lunch/Event = 1 pt.
Send Affiliate Link to 5 People = 2 pts.
1 Hour of Reading or Education = 1 Pt.

Total Points

Afternoon

Tasks That Must be Completed

Afternoon Schedule

Point Value

12PM

12:30

1PM

1:30

2PM

2:30

3PM

3:30

4PM

4:30

5PM

5:30

6PM

Notes For Tomorrow / Appointments after 7PM

Who to connect with today

Daily Reflection

Something I truly appreciated about today was...

I am proud of the way I handled this task or situation today...

Something new I learned today was...
Today could have improved if I...

If I were my own coach, I would tell my-self this about today...

Win The Day Scorecard

score yourself 1-5

Intention
I lived intentionally today according to my "why"

Energy
My physical and mental energy today

Boldness
Today I stepped out of my comfort zone in confidence and authenticity

Essentalism
I prioritized my day according to what mattered most to me

Influence
I made a positive impact on others today

Urgency
I am aware that if I don't help people, they may never be helped.

Weekly Learning Review

Three or more amazing things that happened this week

The main struggle I had this past week was...

If you were coaching yourself, how would you coach yourself to handle this next week?

Two areas I grew in this week were...

Three things I learned about others this week (your loved ones, friends, clients, etc...)

Something I could have done to have more success in the areas that matter to me was...

Weekly Win The Day Review

At the end of every day this past week, you scored yourself according to INTENTION, ENERGY, URGENCY, ESSENTIALISM, INFLUENCE, & BOLDNESS. Add the scores up for each section and include them in the bubbles below. Don't be hard on yourself, but be honest. Take your number and divide by 2. The maximum score you can receive is 105.

Intention	Energy	Essentialism
Urgency	**Influence**	**Boldness**

Dates: __ / __ / __ - __ / __ / __

Total

Weekly Business Reflection

The area I excelled most in this week and why...

Something I could have done this past week to achieve more success...

What I will do differently next week to elevate my performance...

What is the one activity I am not doing enough of?

Who on the team can help me elevate my performance through joint work or mentoring?

Who on the team can I serve or collaborate with in a mutually beneficial way?

What am I most proud of this week?

If you were your own coach, what would you tell yourself you need to do next week to achieve your results?

Weekly Business Point Tracking

Day	Total Points
Monday	
Tuesday	
Wednesday	
Thursday	
Friday	
Saturday	
Sunday	
Total	

Date __ / __ / __

Morning

Morning Mindset

The thing I am most excited about today is...

Something that might disrupt my success today is...

How I will deal with it...

A person who needs my help today is...

Someone I could surprise with an act of kindness today is...

Something I could do to demonstrate excellence or add true value to my community is...

One thing I could do to today that is out of my comfort zone is...

If I was a coach looking at my life, I would remind myself to remember that...

What is the one word I want to describe me as the best version of myself today?

I know today is a major success if...

Today's Top 3 Goals / Priorities

Morning Schedule		Point Value
5AM		
5:30		
6AM		
6:30		
7AM		
7:30		
8AM		
8:30		
9AM		
9:30		
10AM		
10:30		
11AM		

Daily Movement / Health

15 Point Day (Index of values for activities)

Make Appointment = 3 pts.
Have Meeting and schedule Follow Up = 3 pts.
Get Referral = 2 pts.
Application = 5 pts.
Policy Enforce = 5 pts.
Attend Network Event = 2pts.
Take Prospect/Client to Lunch/Event = 1 pt.
Send Affiliate Link to 5 People = 2 pts.
1 Hour of Reading or Education = 1 Pt.

Total Points

Afternoon

Tasks That Must be Completed

Who to connect with today

Afternoon Schedule

Point Value

12PM

12:30

1PM

1:30

2PM

2:30

3PM

3:30

4PM

4:30

5PM

5:30

6PM

Daily Reflection

Something I truly appreciated about today was...

I am proud of the way I handled this task or situation today...

Something new I learned today was...

Today could have improved if I...

If I were my own coach, I would tell myself this about today...

Win The Day Scorecard

score yourself 1-5

Intention
I lived intentionally today according to my "why"

Energy
My physical and mental energy today

Boldness
Today I stepped out of my comfort zone in confidence and authenticity

Essentialism
I prioritized my day according to what mattered most to me

Influence
I made a positive impact on others today

Urgency
I am aware that if I don't help people, they may never be helped.

Notes For Tomorrow / Appointments after 7PM

Date __ /__ / __

Morning

Morning Mindset

The thing I am most excited about today is...

Something that might disrupt my success today is...

How I will deal with it...

A person who needs my help today is...

Someone I could surprise with an act of kindness today is...

Something I could do to demonstrate excellence or add true value to my community is...

One thing I could do to today that is out of my comfort zone is...

If I was a coach looking at my life, I would remind myself to remember that...

What is the one word I want to describe me as the best version of myself today?

I know today is a major success if...

Today's Top 3 Goals / Priorities

Time	Morning Schedule	Point Value
5AM		
5:30		
6AM		
6:30		
7AM		
7:30		
8AM		
8:30		
9AM		
9:30		
10AM		
10:30		
11AM		

Daily Movement / Health

15 Point Day (Index of values for activities)

Make Appointment = 3 pts.
Have Meeting and schedule Follow Up = 3 pts.
Get Referral = 2 pts.
Application = 5 pts.
Policy Enforce = 5 pts.
Attend Network Event = 2pts.
Take Prospect/Client to Lunch/Event = 1 pt.
Send Affiliate Link to 5 People = 2 pts.
1 Hour of Reading or Education = 1 Pt.

Total Points

Afternoon

Tasks That Must be Completed

Who to connect with today

Afternoon Schedule

Point Value

12PM

12:30

1PM

1:30

2PM

2:30

3PM

3:30

4PM

4:30

5PM

5:30

6PM

Notes For Tomorrow / Appointments after 7PM

Daily Reflection

Something I truly appreciated about today was...

I am proud of the way I handled this task or situation today...

Something new I learned today was...

Today could have improved if I...

If I were my own coach, I would tell my-self this about today...

Win The Day Scorecard

score yourself 1-5

Intention
I lived intentionally today according to my "why"

Energy
My physical and mental energy today

Boldness
Today I stepped out of my comfort zone in confidence and authenticity

Essentialism
I prioritized my day according to what mattered most to me

Influence
I made a positive impact on others today

Urgency
I am aware that if I don't help people, they may never be helped.

Date __ / __ / __

Morning

Morning Mindset

The thing I am most excited about today is...

Something that might disrupt my success today is...

How I will deal with it...

A person who needs my help today is...

Someone I could surprise with an act of kindness today is...

Something I could do to demonstrate excellence or add true value to my community is...

One thing I could do to today that is out of my comfort zone is...

If I was a coach looking at my life, I would remind myself to remember that...

What is the one word I want to describe me as the best version of myself today?

I know today is a major success if...

Today's Top 3 Goals / Priorities

Morning Schedule		Point Value
5AM		
5:30		
6AM		
6:30		
7AM		
7:30		
8AM		
8:30		
9AM		
9:30		
10AM		
10:30		
11AM		

Daily Movement / Health

15 Point Day (Index of values for activities)

Make Appointment = 3 pts.
Have Meeting and schedule Follow Up = 3 pts.
Get Referral = 2 pts.
Application = 5 pts.
Policy Enforce = 5 pts.
Attend Network Event = 2pts.
Take Prospect/Client to Lunch/Event = 1 pt.
Send Affiliate Link to 5 People = 2 pts.
1 Hour of Reading or Education = 1 Pt.

Total Points

Afternoon

Tasks That Must be Completed

Who to connect with today

Afternoon Schedule

Point Value

12PM

12:30

1PM

1:30

2PM

2:30

3PM

3:30

4PM

4:30

5PM

5:30

6PM

Daily Reflection

Something I truly appreciated about today was...

I am proud of the way I handled this task or situation today...

Something new I learned today was...

Today could have improved if I...

If I were my own coach, I would tell my-self this about today...

Win The Day Scorecard

score yourself 1-5

Intention
I lived intentionally today according to my "why"

Energy
My physical and mental energy today

Boldness
Today I stepped out of my comfort zone in confidence and authenticity

Essentalism
I prioritized my day according to what mattered most to me

Influence
I made a positive impact on others today

Urgency
I am aware that if I don't help people, they may never be helped.

Notes For Tomorrow / Appointments after 7PM

Date __ /__ / __

Morning

Morning Mindset

The thing I am most excited about today is...

Something that might disrupt my success today is...

How I will deal with it...

A person who needs my help today is...

Someone I could surprise with an act of kindness today is...

Something I could do to demonstrate excellence or add true value to my community is...

One thing I could do to today that is out of my comfort zone is...

If I was a coach looking at my life, I would remind myself to remember that...

What is the one word I want to describe me as the best version of myself today?

I know today is a major success if...

Today's Top 3 Goals / Priorities

Morning Schedule		Point Value
5AM		
5:30		
6AM		
6:30		
7AM		
7:30		
8AM		
8:30		
9AM		
9:30		
10AM		
10:30		
11AM		

Daily Movement / Health

15 Point Day (Index of values for activities)

Make Appointment = 3 pts.
Have Meeting and schedule Follow Up = 3 pts.
Get Referral = 2 pts.
Application = 5 pts.
Policy Enforce = 5 pts.
Attend Network Event = 2pts.
Take Prospect/Client to Lunch/Event = 1 pt.
Send Affiliate Link to 5 People = 2 pts.
1 Hour of Reading or Education = 1 Pt.

Total Points

Afternoon

Tasks That Must be Completed

Who to connect with today

Afternoon Schedule

Point Value

12PM

12:30

1PM

1:30

2PM

2:30

3PM

3:30

4PM

4:30

5PM

5:30

6PM

Notes For Tomorrow / Appointments after 7PM

LIFE180

Daily Reflection

Something I truly appreciated about today was...

I am proud of the way I handled this task or situation today...

Something new I learned today was...
Today could have improved if I...

If I were my own coach, I would tell myself this about today...

Win The Day Scorecard

score yourself 1-5

Intention
I lived intentionally today according to my "why"

Energy
My physical and mental energy today

Boldness
Today I stepped out of my comfort zone in confidence and authenticity

Essentialism
I prioritized my day according to what mattered most to me

Influence
I made a positive impact on others today

Urgency
I am aware that if I don't help people, they may never be helped.

Date __ /__ / __

Morning

Morning Mindset

The thing I am most excited about today is...

Something that might disrupt my success today is...

How I will deal with it...

A person who needs my help today is...

Someone I could surprise with an act of kindness today is...

Something I could do to demonstrate excellence or add true value to my community is...

One thing I could do to today that is out of my comfort zone is...

If I was a coach looking at my life, I would remind myself to remember that...

What is the one word I want to describe me as the best version of myself today?

I know today is a major success if...

Today's Top 3 Goals / Priorities

Morning Schedule		Point Value
5AM		
5:30		
6AM		
6:30		
7AM		
7:30		
8AM		
8:30		
9AM		
9:30		
10AM		
10:30		
11AM		

Daily Movement / Health

15 Point Day (Index of values for activities)

Make Appointment = 3 pts.
Have Meeting and schedule Follow Up = 3 pts.
Get Referral = 2 pts.
Application = 5 pts.
Policy Enforce = 5 pts.
Attend Network Event = 2pts.
Take Prospect/Client to Lunch/Event = 1 pt.
Send Affiliate Link to 5 People = 2 pts.
1 Hour of Reading or Education = 1 Pt.

Total Points

Afternoon

Tasks That Must be Completed

Who to connect with today

Afternoon Schedule

Point Value

12PM

12:30

1PM

1:30

2PM

2:30

3PM

3:30

4PM

4:30

5PM

5:30

6PM

Daily Reflection

Something I truly appreciated about today was...

I am proud of the way I handled this task or situation today...

Something new I learned today was...

Today could have improved if I...

If I were my own coach, I would tell my-self this about today...

Win The Day Scorecard

score yourself 1-5

Intention
I lived intentionally today according to my "why"

Energy
My physical and mental energy today

Boldness
Today I stepped out of my comfort zone in confidence and authenticity

Essentalism
I prioritized my day according to what mattered most to me

Influence
I made a positive impact on others today

Urgency
I am aware that if I don't help people, they may never be helped.

Notes For Tomorrow / Appointments after 7PM

Date __ / __ / __

Morning

Morning Mindset

The thing I am most excited about today is...

Something that might disrupt my success today is...

How I will deal with it...

A person who needs my help today is...

Someone I could surprise with an act of kindness today is...

Something I could do to demonstrate excellence or add true value to my community is...

One thing I could do to today that is out of my comfort zone is...

If I was a coach looking at my life, I would remind myself to remember that...

What is the one word I want to describe me as the best version of myself today?

I know today is a major success if...

Today's Top 3 Goals / Priorities

Morning Schedule		Point Value
5AM		
5:30		
6AM		
6:30		
7AM		
7:30		
8AM		
8:30		
9AM		
9:30		
10AM		
10:30		
11AM		

Daily Movement / Health

15 Point Day (Index of values for activities)

Make Appointment = 3 pts.
Have Meeting and schedule Follow Up = 3 pts.
Get Referral = 2 pts.
Application = 5 pts.
Policy Enforce = 5 pts.
Attend Network Event = 2pts.
Take Prospect/Client to Lunch/Event = 1 pt.
Send Affiliate Link to 5 People = 2 pts.
1 Hour of Reading or Education = 1 Pt.

Total Points

Afternoon

Tasks That Must be Completed

Who to connect with today

Afternoon Schedule

Point Value

12PM

12:30

1PM

1:30

2PM

2:30

3PM

3:30

4PM

4:30

5PM

5:30

6PM

Notes For Tomorrow / Appointments after 7PM

Daily Reflection

Something I truly appreciated about today was...

I am proud of the way I handled this task or situation today...

Something new I learned today was...

Today could have improved if I...

If I were my own coach, I would tell myself this about today...

Win The Day Scorecard

score yourself 1-5

Intention
I lived intentionally today according to my "why"

Energy
My physical and mental energy today

Boldness
Today I stepped out of my comfort zone in confidence and authenticity

Essentialism
I prioritized my day according to what mattered most to me

Influence
I made a positive impact on others today

Urgency
I am aware that if I don't help people, they may never be helped.

Date __ / __ / __

Morning

Morning Mindset

The thing I am most excited about today is...

Something that might disrupt my success today is...

How I will deal with it...

A person who needs my help today is...

Someone I could surprise with an act of kindness today is...

Something I could do to demonstrate excellence or add true value to my community is...

One thing I could do to today that is out of my comfort zone is...

If I was a coach looking at my life, I would remind myself to remember that...

What is the one word I want to describe me as the best version of myself today?

I know today is a major success if...

Today's Top 3 Goals / Priorities

Morning Schedule		Point Value
5AM		
5:30		
6AM		
6:30		
7AM		
7:30		
8AM		
8:30		
9AM		
9:30		
10AM		
10:30		
11AM		

Daily Movement / Health

15 Point Day (Index of values for activities)

Make Appointment = 3 pts.
Have Meeting and schedule Follow Up = 3 pts.
Get Referral = 2 pts.
Application = 5 pts.
Policy Enforce = 5 pts.
Attend Network Event = 2pts.
Take Prospect/Client to Lunch/Event = 1 pt.
Send Affiliate Link to 5 People = 2 pts.
1 Hour of Reading or Education = 1 Pt.

Total Points

Afternoon

Tasks That Must be Completed

Who to connect with today

Afternoon Schedule

Point Value

12PM

12:30

1PM

1:30

2PM

2:30

3PM

3:30

4PM

4:30

5PM

5:30

6PM

Daily Reflection

Something I truly appreciated about today was...

I am proud of the way I handled this task or situation today...

Something new I learned today was...

Today could have improved if I...

If I were my own coach, I would tell myself this about today...

Win The Day Scorecard

score yourself 1-5

Intention
I lived intentionally today according to my "why"

Energy
My physical and mental energy today

Boldness
Today I stepped out of my comfort zone in confidence and authenticity

Essentialism
I prioritized my day according to what mattered most to me

Influence
I made a positive impact on others today

Urgency
I am aware that if I don't help people, they may never be helped.

Notes For Tomorrow / Appointments after 7PM

Weekly Learning Review

Three or more amazing things that happened this week

The main struggle I had this past week was...

If you were coaching yourself, how would you coach yourself to handle this next week?

Two areas I grew in this week were...

Three things I learned about others this week (your loved ones, friends, clients, etc...)

Something I could have done to have more success in the areas that matter to me was...

Weekly Win The Day Review

At the end of every day this past week, you scored yourself according to INTENTION, ENERGY, URGENCY, ESSENTIALISM, INFLUENCE, & BOLDNESS. Add the scores up for each section and include them in the bubbles below. Don't be hard on yourself, but be honest. Take your number and divide by 2. The maximum score you can receive is 105.

Intention	Energy	Essentialism
Urgency	**Influence**	**Boldness**

Dates: __/__/__ - __/__/__

Total	

Weekly Business Reflection

The area I excelled most in this week and why...

Something I could have done this past week to achieve more success...

What I will do differently next week to elevate my performance...

What is the one activity I am not doing enough of?

Who on the team can help me elevate my performance through joint work or mentoring?

Who on the team can I serve or collaborate with in a mutually beneficial way?

What am I most proud of this week?

If you were your own coach, what would you tell yourself you need to do next week to achieve your results?

Weekly Business Point Tracking

Day	Total Points
Monday	
Tuesday	
Wednesday	
Thursday	
Friday	
Saturday	
Sunday	
Total	

Date __ / __ / __

Morning

Morning Mindset

The thing I am most excited about today is...

Something that might disrupt my success today is...

How I will deal with it...

A person who needs my help today is...

Someone I could surprise with an act of kindness today is...

Something I could do to demonstrate excellence or add true value to my community is...

One thing I could do to today that is out of my comfort zone is...

If I was a coach looking at my life, I would remind myself to remember that...

What is the one word I want to describe me as the best version of myself today?

I know today is a major success if...

Today's Top 3 Goals / Priorities

Morning Schedule		Point Value
5AM		
5:30		
6AM		
6:30		
7AM		
7:30		
8AM		
8:30		
9AM		
9:30		
10AM		
10:30		
11AM		

Daily Movement / Health

15 Point Day (Index of values for activities)

Make Appointment = 3 pts.
Have Meeting and schedule Follow Up = 3 pts.
Get Referral = 2 pts.
Application = 5 pts.
Policy Enforce = 5 pts.
Attend Network Event = 2pts.
Take Prospect/Client to Lunch/Event = 1 pt.
Send Affiliate Link to 5 People = 2 pts.
1 Hour of Reading or Education = 1 Pt.

Total Points

Afternoon

Tasks That Must be Completed

Who to connect with today

Afternoon Schedule

Point Value

12PM

12:30

1PM

1:30

2PM

2:30

3PM

3:30

4PM

4:30

5PM

5:30

6PM

Notes For Tomorrow / Appointments after 7PM

LIFE180

Daily Reflection

Something I truly appreciated about today was...

I am proud of the way I handled this task or situation today...

Something new I learned today was...
Today could have improved if I...

If I were my own coach, I would tell my-self this about today...

Win The Day Scorecard

score yourself 1-5

Intention
I lived intentionally today according to my "why"

Energy
My physical and mental energy today

Boldness
Today I stepped out of my comfort zone in confidence and authenticity

Essentialism
I prioritized my day according to what mattered most to me

Influence
I made a positive impact on others today

Urgency
I am aware that if I don't help people, they may never be helped.

Date __ / __ / __

Morning

Morning Mindset

The thing I am most excited about today is...

Something that might disrupt my success today is...

How I will deal with it...

A person who needs my help today is...

Someone I could surprise with an act of kindness today is...

Something I could do to demonstrate excellence or add true value to my community is...

One thing I could do to today that is out of my comfort zone is...

If I was a coach looking at my life, I would remind myself to remember that...

What is the one word I want to describe me as the best version of myself today?

I know today is a major success if...

Today's Top 3 Goals / Priorities

Morning Schedule		Point Value
5AM		
5:30		
6AM		
6:30		
7AM		
7:30		
8AM		
8:30		
9AM		
9:30		
10AM		
10:30		
11AM		

Daily Movement / Health

15 Point Day (Index of values for activities)

Make Appointment = 3 pts.
Have Meeting and schedule Follow Up = 3 pts.
Get Referral = 2 pts.
Application = 5 pts.
Policy Enforce = 5 pts.
Attend Network Event = 2pts.
Take Prospect/Client to Lunch/Event = 1 pt.
Send Affiliate Link to 5 People = 2 pts.
1 Hour of Reading or Education = 1 Pt.

Total Points

Afternoon

Tasks That Must be Completed

Who to connect with today

Afternoon Schedule

Point Value

12PM

12:30

1PM

1:30

2PM

2:30

3PM

3:30

4PM

4:30

5PM

5:30

6PM

Daily Reflection

Something I truly appreciated about today was...

I am proud of the way I handled this task or situation today...

Something new I learned today was...

Today could have improved if I...

If I were my own coach, I would tell myself this about today...

Notes For Tomorrow / Appointments after 7PM

LIFE180

Win The Day Scorecard

score yourself 1-5

Intention
I lived intentionally today according to my "why"

Energy
My physical and mental energy today

Boldness
Today I stepped out of my comfort zone in confidence and authenticity

Essentialism
I prioritized my day according to what mattered most to me

Influence
I made a positive impact on others today

Urgency
I am aware that if I don't help people, they may never be helped.

Date __ /__ / __

Morning

Morning Mindset

The thing I am most excited about today is...

Something that might disrupt my success today is...

How I will deal with it...

A person who needs my help today is...

Someone I could surprise with an act of kindness today is...

Something I could do to demonstrate excellence or add true value to my community is...

One thing I could do to today that is out of my comfort zone is...

If I was a coach looking at my life, I would remind myself to remember that...

What is the one word I want to describe me as the best version of myself today?

I know today is a major success if...

Today's Top 3 Goals / Priorities

Time	Morning Schedule	Point Value
5AM		
5:30		
6AM		
6:30		
7AM		
7:30		
8AM		
8:30		
9AM		
9:30		
10AM		
10:30		
11AM		

Daily Movement / Health

15 Point Day (Index of values for activities)

Make Appointment = 3 pts.
Have Meeting and schedule Follow Up = 3 pts.
Get Referral = 2 pts.
Application = 5 pts.
Policy Enforce = 5 pts.
Attend Network Event = 2pts.
Take Prospect/Client to Lunch/Event = 1 pt.
Send Affiliate Link to 5 People = 2 pts.
1 Hour of Reading or Education = 1 Pt.

Total Points

Afternoon

Tasks That Must be Completed

Who to connect with today

Afternoon Schedule

Point Value

12PM

12:30

1PM

1:30

2PM

2:30

3PM

3:30

4PM

4:30

5PM

5:30

6PM

Notes For Tomorrow / Appointments after 7PM

LIFE180

Daily Reflection

Something I truly appreciated about today was...

I am proud of the way I handled this task or situation today...

Something new I learned today was...

Today could have improved if I...

If I were my own coach, I would tell myself this about today...

Win The Day Scorecard

score yourself 1-5

Intention
I lived intentionally today according to my "why"

Energy
My physical and mental energy today

Boldness
Today I stepped out of my comfort zone in confidence and authenticity

Essentialism
I prioritized my day according to what mattered most to me

Influence
I made a positive impact on others today

Urgency
I am aware that if I don't help people, they may never be helped.

Date __ / __ / __

Morning

Morning Mindset

The thing I am most excited about today is...

Something that might disrupt my success today is...

How I will deal with it...

A person who needs my help today is...

Someone I could surprise with an act of kindness today is...

Something I could do to demonstrate excellence or add true value to my community is...

One thing I could do to today that is out of my comfort zone is...

If I was a coach looking at my life, I would remind myself to remember that...

What is the one word I want to describe me as the best version of myself today?

I know today is a major success if...

Today's Top 3 Goals / Priorities

Morning Schedule		Point Value
5AM		
5:30		
6AM		
6:30		
7AM		
7:30		
8AM		
8:30		
9AM		
9:30		
10AM		
10:30		
11AM		

Daily Movement / Health

15 Point Day (Index of values for activities)

Make Appointment = 3 pts.
Have Meeting and schedule Follow Up = 3 pts.
Get Referral = 2 pts.
Application = 5 pts.
Policy Enforce = 5 pts.
Attend Network Event = 2pts.
Take Prospect/Client to Lunch/Event = 1 pt.
Send Affiliate Link to 5 People = 2 pts.
1 Hour of Reading or Education = 1 Pt.

Total Points

Afternoon

Tasks That Must be Completed

Who to connect with today

Afternoon Schedule

Point Value

12PM

12:30

1PM

1:30

2PM

2:30

3PM

3:30

4PM

4:30

5PM

5:30

6PM

Daily Reflection

Something I truly appreciated about today was...

I am proud of the way I handled this task or situation today...

Something new I learned today was...

Today could have improved if I...

If I were my own coach, I would tell myself this about today...

Win The Day Scorecard

score yourself 1-5

Intention
I lived intentionally today according to my "why"

Energy
My physical and mental energy today

Boldness
Today I stepped out of my comfort zone in confidence and authenticity

Essentalism
I prioritized my day according to what mattered most to me

Influence
I made a positive impact on others today

Urgency
I am aware that if I don't help people, they may never be helped.

Notes For Tomorrow / Appointments after 7PM

Date __ / __ / __

Morning

Morning Mindset

The thing I am most excited about today is...

Something that might disrupt my success today is...

How I will deal with it...

A person who needs my help today is...

Someone I could surprise with an act of kindness today is...

Something I could do to demonstrate excellence or add true value to my community is...

One thing I could do to today that is out of my comfort zone is...

If I was a coach looking at my life, I would remind myself to remember that...

What is the one word I want to describe me as the best version of myself today?

I know today is a major success if...

Today's Top 3 Goals / Priorities

Morning Schedule		Point Value
5AM		
5:30		
6AM		
6:30		
7AM		
7:30		
8AM		
8:30		
9AM		
9:30		
10AM		
10:30		
11AM		

Daily Movement / Health

15 Point Day (Index of values for activities)

Make Appointment = 3 pts.
Have Meeting and schedule Follow Up = 3 pts.
Get Referral = 2 pts.
Application = 5 pts.
Policy Enforce = 5 pts.
Attend Network Event = 2pts.
Take Prospect/Client to Lunch/Event = 1 pt.
Send Affiliate Link to 5 People = 2 pts.
1 Hour of Reading or Education = 1 Pt.

Total Points

Afternoon

Tasks That Must be Completed

Who to connect with today

Afternoon Schedule

Point Value

12PM

12:30

1PM

1:30

2PM

2:30

3PM

3:30

4PM

4:30

5PM

5:30

6PM

Notes For Tomorrow / Appointments after 7PM

Daily Reflection

Something I truly appreciated about today was...

I am proud of the way I handled this task or situation today...

Something new I learned today was...
Today could have improved if I...

If I were my own coach, I would tell myself this about today...

Win The Day Scorecard

score yourself 1-5

Intention
I lived intentionally today according to my "why"

Energy
My physical and mental energy today

Boldness
Today I stepped out of my comfort zone in confidence and authenticity

Essentialism
I prioritized my day according to what mattered most to me

Influence
I made a positive impact on others today

Urgency
I am aware that if I don't help people, they may never be helped.

Date __ /__ / __

Morning

Morning Mindset

The thing I am most excited about today is...

Something that might disrupt my success today is...

How I will deal with it...

A person who needs my help today is...

Someone I could surprise with an act of kindness today is...

Something I could do to demonstrate excellence or add true value to my community is...

One thing I could do to today that is out of my comfort zone is...

If I was a coach looking at my life, I would remind myself to remember that...

What is the one word I want to describe me as the best version of myself today?

I know today is a major success if...

Today's Top 3 Goals / Priorities

Morning Schedule		Point Value
5AM		
5:30		
6AM		
6:30		
7AM		
7:30		
8AM		
8:30		
9AM		
9:30		
10AM		
10:30		
11AM		

Daily Movement / Health

15 Point Day (Index of values for activities)

Make Appointment = 3 pts.
Have Meeting and schedule Follow Up = 3 pts.
Get Referral = 2 pts.
Application = 5 pts.
Policy Enforce = 5 pts.
Attend Network Event = 2pts.
Take Prospect/Client to Lunch/Event = 1 pt.
Send Affiliate Link to 5 People = 2 pts.
1 Hour of Reading or Education = 1 Pt.

Total Points

Afternoon

Tasks That Must be Completed

Who to connect with today

Afternoon Schedule

Point Value

12PM

12:30

1PM

1:30

2PM

2:30

3PM

3:30

4PM

4:30

5PM

5:30

6PM

Notes For Tomorrow / Appointments after 7PM

LIFE180

Daily Reflection

Something I truly appreciated about today was...

I am proud of the way I handled this task or situation today...

Something new I learned today was...

Today could have improved if I...

If I were my own coach, I would tell myself this about today...

Win The Day Scorecard

score yourself 1-5

Intention
I lived intentionally today according to my "why"

Energy
My physical and mental energy today

Boldness
Today I stepped out of my comfort zone in confidence and authenticity

Essentialism
I prioritized my day according to what mattered most to me

Influence
I made a positive impact on others today

Urgency
I am aware that if I don't help people, they may never be helped.

Date __ /__ / __

Morning

Morning Mindset

The thing I am most excited about today is...

Something that might disrupt my success today is...

How I will deal with it...

A person who needs my help today is...

Someone I could surprise with an act of kindness today is...

Something I could do to demonstrate excellence or add true value to my community is...

One thing I could do to today that is out of my comfort zone is...

If I was a coach looking at my life, I would remind myself to remember that...

What is the one word I want to describe me as the best version of myself today?

I know today is a major success if...

Today's Top 3 Goals / Priorities

Morning Schedule		Point Value
5AM		
5:30		
6AM		
6:30		
7AM		
7:30		
8AM		
8:30		
9AM		
9:30		
10AM		
10:30		
11AM		

Daily Movement / Health

15 Point Day (Index of values for activities)

Make Appointment = 3 pts.
Have Meeting and schedule Follow Up = 3 pts.
Get Referral = 2 pts.
Application = 5 pts.
Policy Enforce = 5 pts.
Attend Network Event = 2pts.
Take Prospect/Client to Lunch/Event = 1 pt.
Send Affiliate Link to 5 People = 2 pts.
1 Hour of Reading or Education = 1 Pt.

Total Points

Afternoon

Tasks That Must be Completed

Afternoon Schedule

Point Value

12PM

12:30

1PM

1:30

2PM

2:30

3PM

3:30

4PM

4:30

5PM

5:30

6PM

Notes For Tomorrow / Appointments after 7PM

LIFE180

Who to connect with today

Daily Reflection

Something I truly appreciated about today was...

I am proud of the way I handled this task or situation today...

Something new I learned today was...
Today could have improved if I...

If I were my own coach, I would tell myself this about today...

Win The Day Scorecard

score yourself 1-5

Intention
I lived intentionally today according to my "why"

Energy
My physical and mental energy today

Boldness
Today I stepped out of my comfort zone in confidence and authenticity

Essentialism
I prioritized my day according to what mattered most to me

Influence
I made a positive impact on others today

Urgency
I am aware that if I don't help people, they may never be helped.

Weekly Learning Review

Three or more amazing things that happened this week

The main struggle I had this past week was...

If you were coaching yourself, how would you coach yourself to handle this next week?

Two areas I grew in this week were...

Three things I learned about others this week (your loved ones, friends, clients, etc...)

Something I could have done to have more success in the areas that matter to me was...

Weekly Win The Day Review

At the end of every day this past week, you scored yourself according to INTENTION, ENERGY, URGENCY, ESSENTIALISM, INFLUENCE, & BOLDNESS. Add the scores up for each section and include them in the bubbles below. Don't be hard on yourself, but be honest. Take your number and divide by 2. The maximum score you can receive is 105.

Intention	Energy	Essentialism
Urgency	**Influence**	**Boldness**

Dates: _ _ / _ _ / _ _ - _ _ / _ _ / _ _

Total	

Weekly Business Reflection

The area I excelled most in this week and why...

Something I could have done this past week to achieve more success...

What I will do differently next week to elevate my performance...

What is the one activity I am not doing enough of?

Who on the team can help me elevate my performance through joint work or mentoring?

Who on the team can I serve or collaborate with in a mutually beneficial way?

What am I most proud of this week?

If you were your own coach, what would you tell yourself you need to do next week to achieve your results?

Weekly Business Point Tracking

Day	Total Points
Monday	
Tuesday	
Wednesday	
Thursday	
Friday	
Saturday	
Sunday	
Total	

Date __ / __ / __

Morning

Morning Mindset

The thing I am most excited about today is...

Something that might disrupt my success today is...

How I will deal with it...

A person who needs my help today is...

Someone I could surprise with an act of kindness today is...

Something I could do to demonstrate excellence or add true value to my community is...

One thing I could do to today that is out of my comfort zone is...

If I was a coach looking at my life, I would remind myself to remember that...

What is the one word I want to describe me as the best version of myself today?

I know today is a major success if...

Today's Top 3 Goals / Priorities

	Morning Schedule	Point Value
5AM		
5:30		
6AM		
6:30		
7AM		
7:30		
8AM		
8:30		
9AM		
9:30		
10AM		
10:30		
11AM		

Daily Movement / Health

15 Point Day (Index of values for activities)

Make Appointment = 3 pts.
Have Meeting and schedule Follow Up = 3 pts.
Get Referral = 2 pts.
Application = 5 pts.
Policy Enforce = 5 pts.
Attend Network Event = 2pts.
Take Prospect/Client to Lunch/Event = 1 pt.
Send Affiliate Link to 5 People = 2 pts.
1 Hour of Reading or Education = 1 Pt.

Total Points

Afternoon

Tasks That Must be Completed

Who to connect with today

Afternoon Schedule | Point Value

12PM

12:30

1PM

1:30

2PM

2:30

3PM

3:30

4PM

4:30

5PM

5:30

6PM

Notes For Tomorrow / Appointments after 7PM

Daily Reflection

Something I truly appreciated about today was...

I am proud of the way I handled this task or situation today...

Something new I learned today was...
Today could have improved if I...

If I were my own coach, I would tell myself this about today...

Win The Day Scorecard

score yourself 1-5

Intention
I lived intentionally today according to my "why"

Energy
My physical and mental energy today

Boldness
Today I stepped out of my comfort zone in confidence and authenticity

Essentialism
I prioritized my day according to what mattered most to me

Influence
I made a positive impact on others today

Urgency
I am aware that if I don't help people, they may never be helped.

Date __ /__ / __

Morning

Morning Mindset

The thing I am most excited about today is...

Something that might disrupt my success today is...

How I will deal with it...

A person who needs my help today is...

Someone I could surprise with an act of kindness today is...

Something I could do to demonstrate excellence or add true value to my community is...

One thing I could do to today that is out of my comfort zone is...

If I was a coach looking at my life, I would remind myself to remember that...

What is the one word I want to describe me as the best version of myself today?

I know today is a major success if...

Today's Top 3 Goals / Priorities

Morning Schedule		Point Value
5AM		
5:30		
6AM		
6:30		
7AM		
7:30		
8AM		
8:30		
9AM		
9:30		
10AM		
10:30		
11AM		

Daily Movement / Health

15 Point Day (Index of values for activities)

Make Appointment = 3 pts.
Have Meeting and schedule Follow Up = 3 pts.
Get Referral = 2 pts.
Application = 5 pts.
Policy Enforce = 5 pts.
Attend Network Event = 2pts.
Take Prospect/Client to Lunch/Event = 1 pt.
Send Affiliate Link to 5 People = 2 pts.
1 Hour of Reading or Education = 1 Pt.

Total Points

Afternoon

Tasks That Must be Completed

Who to connect with today

Afternoon Schedule

Point Value

12PM

12:30

1PM

1:30

2PM

2:30

3PM

3:30

4PM

4:30

5PM

5:30

6PM

Daily Reflection

Something I truly appreciated about today was...

I am proud of the way I handled this task or situation today...

Something new I learned today was...

Today could have improved if I...

If I were my own coach, I would tell myself this about today...

Win The Day Scorecard

score yourself 1-5

Intention
I lived intentionally today according to my "why"

Energy
My physical and mental energy today

Boldness
Today I stepped out of my comfort zone in confidence and authenticity

Essentialism
I prioritized my day according to what mattered most to me

Influence
I made a positive impact on others today

Urgency
I am aware that if I don't help people, they may never be helped.

Notes For Tomorrow / Appointments after 7PM

Date __ /__ / __

Morning

Morning Mindset

The thing I am most excited about today is...

Something that might disrupt my success today is...

How I will deal with it...

A person who needs my help today is...

Someone I could surprise with an act of kindness today is...

Something I could do to demonstrate excellence or add true value to my community is...

One thing I could do to today that is out of my comfort zone is...

If I was a coach looking at my life, I would remind myself to remember that...

What is the one word I want to describe me as the best version of myself today?

I know today is a major success if...

Today's Top 3 Goals / Priorities

Morning Schedule		Point Value
5AM		
5:30		
6AM		
6:30		
7AM		
7:30		
8AM		
8:30		
9AM		
9:30		
10AM		
10:30		
11AM		

Daily Movement / Health

15 Point Day (Index of values for activities)

Make Appointment = 3 pts.
Have Meeting and schedule Follow Up = 3 pts.
Get Referral = 2 pts.
Application = 5 pts.
Policy Enforce = 5 pts.
Attend Network Event = 2pts.
Take Prospect/Client to Lunch/Event = 1 pt.
Send Affiliate Link to 5 People = 2 pts.
1 Hour of Reading or Education = 1 Pt.

Total Points

Afternoon

Tasks That Must be Completed

Who to connect with today

Afternoon Schedule

Point Value

12PM

12:30

1PM

1:30

2PM

2:30

3PM

3:30

4PM

4:30

5PM

5:30

6PM

Notes For Tomorrow / Appointments after 7PM

Daily Reflection

Something I truly appreciated about today was...

I am proud of the way I handled this task or situation today...

Something new I learned today was...
Today could have improved if I...

If I were my own coach, I would tell myself this about today...

Win The Day Scorecard

score yourself 1-5

Intention
I lived intentionally today according to my "why"

Energy
My physical and mental energy today

Boldness
Today I stepped out of my comfort zone in confidence and authenticity

Essentialism
I prioritized my day according to what mattered most to me

Influence
I made a positive impact on others today

Urgency
I am aware that if I don't help people, they may never be helped.

Date __ / __ / __

Morning

Morning Mindset

The thing I am most excited about today is...

Something that might disrupt my success today is...

How I will deal with it...

A person who needs my help today is...

Someone I could surprise with an act of kindness today is...

Something I could do to demonstrate excellence or add true value to my community is...

One thing I could do to today that is out of my comfort zone is...

If I was a coach looking at my life, I would remind myself to remember that...

What is the one word I want to describe me as the best version of myself today?

I know today is a major success if...

Today's Top 3 Goals / Priorities

Morning Schedule		Point Value
5AM		
5:30		
6AM		
6:30		
7AM		
7:30		
8AM		
8:30		
9AM		
9:30		
10AM		
10:30		
11AM		

Daily Movement / Health

15 Point Day (Index of values for activities)

Make Appointment = 3 pts.
Have Meeting and schedule Follow Up = 3 pts.
Get Referral = 2 pts.
Application = 5 pts.
Policy Enforce = 5 pts.
Attend Network Event = 2pts.
Take Prospect/Client to Lunch/Event = 1 pt.
Send Affiliate Link to 5 People = 2 pts.
1 Hour of Reading or Education = 1 Pt.

Total Points

Afternoon

Tasks That Must be Completed

Who to connect with today

Afternoon Schedule

Point Value

12PM

12:30

1PM

1:30

2PM

2:30

3PM

3:30

4PM

4:30

5PM

5:30

6PM

Daily Reflection

Something I truly appreciated about today was...

I am proud of the way I handled this task or situation today...

Something new I learned today was...

Today could have improved if I...

If I were my own coach, I would tell my-self this about today...

Win The Day Scorecard

score yourself 1-5

Intention
I lived intentionally today according to my "why"

Energy
My physical and mental energy today

Boldness
Today I stepped out of my comfort zone in confidence and authenticity

Essentalism
I prioritized my day according to what mattered most to me

Influence
I made a positive impact on others today

Urgency
I am aware that if I don't help people, they may never be helped.

Notes For Tomorrow / Appointments after 7PM

Date __ /__ / __

Morning

Morning Mindset

The thing I am most excited about today is...

Something that might disrupt my success today is...

How I will deal with it...

A person who needs my help today is...

Someone I could surprise with an act of kindness today is...

Something I could do to demonstrate excellence or add true value to my community is...

One thing I could do to today that is out of my comfort zone is...

If I was a coach looking at my life, I would remind myself to remember that...

What is the one word I want to describe me as the best version of myself today?

I know today is a major success if...

Today's Top 3 Goals / Priorities

Morning Schedule		Point Value
5AM		
5:30		
6AM		
6:30		
7AM		
7:30		
8AM		
8:30		
9AM		
9:30		
10AM		
10:30		
11AM		

LIFE180

Daily Movement / Health

15 Point Day (Index of values for activities)

Make Appointment = 3 pts.
Have Meeting and schedule Follow Up = 3 pts.
Get Referral = 2 pts.
Application = 5 pts.
Policy Enforce = 5 pts.
Attend Network Event = 2pts.
Take Prospect/Client to Lunch/Event = 1 pt.
Send Affiliate Link to 5 People = 2 pts.
1 Hour of Reading or Education = 1 Pt.

Total Points

Afternoon

Tasks That Must be Completed

Who to connect with today

Afternoon Schedule

Point Value

12PM

12:30

1PM

1:30

2PM

2:30

3PM

3:30

4PM

4:30

5PM

5:30

6PM

Notes For Tomorrow / Appointments after 7PM

Daily Reflection

Something I truly appreciated about today was...

I am proud of the way I handled this task or situation today...

Something new I learned today was...
Today could have improved if I...

If I were my own coach, I would tell my-self this about today...

Win The Day Scorecard

score yourself 1-5

Intention
I lived intentionally today according to my "why"

Energy
My physical and mental energy today

Boldness
Today I stepped out of my comfort zone in confidence and authenticity

Essentalism
I prioritized my day according to what mattered most to me

Influence
I made a positive impact on others today

Urgency
I am aware that if I don't help people, they may never be helped.

Date __ / __ / __

Morning

Morning Mindset

The thing I am most excited about today is...

Something that might disrupt my success today is...

How I will deal with it...

A person who needs my help today is...

Someone I could surprise with an act of kindness today is...

Something I could do to demonstrate excellence or add true value to my community is...

One thing I could do to today that is out of my comfort zone is...

If I was a coach looking at my life, I would remind myself to remember that...

What is the one word I want to describe me as the best version of myself today?

I know today is a major success if...

Today's Top 3 Goals / Priorities

	Morning Schedule	Point Value
5AM		
5:30		
6AM		
6:30		
7AM		
7:30		
8AM		
8:30		
9AM		
9:30		
10AM		
10:30		
11AM		

Daily Movement / Health

15 Point Day (Index of values for activities)

Make Appointment = 3 pts.
Have Meeting and schedule Follow Up = 3 pts.
Get Referral = 2 pts.
Application = 5 pts.
Policy Enforce = 5 pts.
Attend Network Event = 2pts.
Take Prospect/Client to Lunch/Event = 1 pt.
Send Affiliate Link to 5 People = 2 pts.
1 Hour of Reading or Education = 1 Pt.

Total Points

Afternoon

Tasks That Must be Completed

Afternoon Schedule

Point Value

12PM

12:30

1PM

1:30

2PM

2:30

3PM

3:30

4PM

4:30

5PM

5:30

6PM

Notes For Tomorrow / Appointments after 7PM

Who to connect with today

Daily Reflection

Something I truly appreciated about today was...

I am proud of the way I handled this task or situation today...

Something new I learned today was...

Today could have improved if I...

If I were my own coach, I would tell myself this about today...

Win The Day Scorecard

score yourself 1-5

Intention
I lived intentionally today according to my "why"

Energy
My physical and mental energy today

Boldness
Today I stepped out of my comfort zone in confidence and authenticity

Essentalism
I prioritized my day according to what mattered most to me

Influence
I made a positive impact on others today

Urgency
I am aware that if I don't help people, they may never be helped.

Date __ /__ / __

Morning

Morning Mindset

The thing I am most excited about today is...

Something that might disrupt my success today is...

How I will deal with it...

A person who needs my help today is...

Someone I could surprise with an act of kindness today is...

Something I could do to demonstrate excellence or add true value to my community is...

One thing I could do to today that is out of my comfort zone is...

If I was a coach looking at my life, I would remind myself to remember that...

What is the one word I want to describe me as the best version of myself today?

I know today is a major success if...

Today's Top 3 Goals / Priorities

Morning Schedule		Point Value
5AM		
5:30		
6AM		
6:30		
7AM		
7:30		
8AM		
8:30		
9AM		
9:30		
10AM		
10:30		
11AM		

Daily Movement / Health

15 Point Day (Index of values for activities)

Make Appointment = 3 pts.
Have Meeting and schedule Follow Up = 3 pts.
Get Referral = 2 pts.
Application = 5 pts.
Policy Enforce = 5 pts.
Attend Network Event = 2pts.
Take Prospect/Client to Lunch/Event = 1 pt.
Send Affiliate Link to 5 People = 2 pts.
1 Hour of Reading or Education = 1 Pt.

Total Points

Afternoon

Tasks That Must be Completed

Who to connect with today

Afternoon Schedule

Point Value

12PM

12:30

1PM

1:30

2PM

2:30

3PM

3:30

4PM

4:30

5PM

5:30

6PM

Notes For Tomorrow / Appointments after 7PM

Daily Reflection

Something I truly appreciated about today was...

I am proud of the way I handled this task or situation today...

Something new I learned today was...
Today could have improved if I...

If I were my own coach, I would tell myself this about today...

Win The Day Scorecard

score yourself 1-5

Intention
I lived intentionally today according to my "why"

Energy
My physical and mental energy today

Boldness
Today I stepped out of my comfort zone in confidence and authenticity

Essentalism
I prioritized my day according to what mattered most to me

Influence
I made a positive impact on others today

Urgency
I am aware that if I don't help people, they may never be helped.

Weekly Learning Review

Three or more amazing things that happened this week

The main struggle I had this past week was...

If you were coaching yourself, how would you coach yourself to handle this next week?

Two areas I grew in this week were...

Three things I learned about others this week (your loved ones, friends, clients, etc...)

Something I could have done to have more success in the areas that matter to me was...

Weekly Win The Day Review

At the end of every day this past week, you scored yourself according to INTENTION, ENERGY, URGENCY, ESSENTIALISM, INFLUENCE, & BOLDNESS. Add the scores up for each section and include them in the bubbles below. Don't be hard on yourself, but be honest. Take your number and divide by 2. The maximum score you can receive is 105.

Intention	Energy	Essentialism
Urgency	Influence	Boldness

Dates: __/__/__ - __/__/__

Total	

Weekly Business Reflection

The area I excelled most in this week and why...

Something I could have done this past week to achieve more success...

What I will do differently next week to elevate my performance...

What is the one activity I am not doing enough of?

Who on the team can help me elevate my performance through joint work or mentoring?

Who on the team can I serve or collaborate with in a mutually beneficial way?

What am I most proud of this week?

If you were your own coach, what would you tell yourself you need to do next week to achieve your results?

Weekly Business Point Tracking

Day	Total Points
Monday	
Tuesday	
Wednesday	
Thursday	
Friday	
Saturday	
Sunday	
Total	

Date __ /__ / __

Morning

Morning Mindset

The thing I am most excited about today is...

Something that might disrupt my success today is...

How I will deal with it...

A person who needs my help today is...

Someone I could surprise with an act of kindness today is...

Something I could do to demonstrate excellence or add true value to my community is...

One thing I could do to today that is out of my comfort zone is...

If I was a coach looking at my life, I would remind myself to remember that...

What is the one word I want to describe me as the best version of myself today?

I know today is a major success if...

Today's Top 3 Goals / Priorities

Morning Schedule

Time	Morning Schedule	Point Value
5AM		
5:30		
6AM		
6:30		
7AM		
7:30		
8AM		
8:30		
9AM		
9:30		
10AM		
10:30		
11AM		

Daily Movement / Health

15 Point Day (Index of values for activities)

Make Appointment = 3 pts.
Have Meeting and schedule Follow Up = 3 pts.
Get Referral = 2 pts.
Application = 5 pts.
Policy Enforce = 5 pts.
Attend Network Event = 2pts.
Take Prospect/Client to Lunch/Event = 1 pt.
Send Affiliate Link to 5 People = 2 pts.
1 Hour of Reading or Education = 1 Pt.

Total Points

Afternoon

Tasks That Must be Completed

Afternoon Schedule — Point Value

12PM

12:30

1PM

1:30

2PM

2:30

3PM

3:30

4PM

4:30

5PM

5:30

6PM

Notes For Tomorrow / Appointments after 7PM

Who to connect with today

Daily Reflection

Something I truly appreciated about today was...

I am proud of the way I handled this task or situation today...

Something new I learned today was...
Today could have improved if I...

If I were my own coach, I would tell myself this about today...

Win The Day Scorecard

score yourself 1-5

Intention
I lived intentionally today according to my "why"

Energy
My physical and mental energy today

Boldness
Today I stepped out of my comfort zone in confidence and authenticity

Essentialism
I prioritized my day according to what mattered most to me

Influence
I made a positive impact on others today

Urgency
I am aware that if I don't help people, they may never be helped.

Date __ / __ / __

Morning

Morning Mindset

The thing I am most excited about today is...

Something that might disrupt my success today is...

How I will deal with it...

A person who needs my help today is...

Someone I could surprise with an act of kindness today is...

Something I could do to demonstrate excellence or add true value to my community is...

One thing I could do to today that is out of my comfort zone is...

If I was a coach looking at my life, I would remind myself to remember that...

What is the one word I want to describe me as the best version of myself today?

I know today is a major success if...

Today's Top 3 Goals / Priorities

Morning Schedule		Point Value
5AM		
5:30		
6AM		
6:30		
7AM		
7:30		
8AM		
8:30		
9AM		
9:30		
10AM		
10:30		
11AM		

Daily Movement / Health

15 Point Day (Index of values for activities)

Make Appointment = 3 pts.
Have Meeting and schedule Follow Up = 3 pts.
Get Referral = 2 pts.
Application = 5 pts.
Policy Enforce = 5 pts.
Attend Network Event = 2pts.
Take Prospect/Client to Lunch/Event = 1 pt.
Send Affiliate Link to 5 People = 2 pts.
1 Hour of Reading or Education = 1 Pt.

Total Points

Afternoon

Tasks That Must be Completed

Afternoon Schedule

Point Value

12PM

12:30

1PM

1:30

2PM

2:30

3PM

3:30

4PM

4:30

5PM

5:30

6PM

Notes For Tomorrow / Appointments after 7PM

Who to connect with today

Daily Reflection

Something I truly appreciated about today was...

I am proud of the way I handled this task or situation today...

Something new I learned today was...
Today could have improved if I...

If I were my own coach, I would tell my-self this about today...

Win The Day Scorecard

score yourself 1-5

Intention
I lived intentionally today according to my "why"

Energy
My physical and mental energy today

Boldness
Today I stepped out of my comfort zone in confidence and authenticity

Essentalism
I prioritized my day according to what mattered most to me

Influence
I made a positive impact on others today

Urgency
I am aware that if I don't help people, they may never be helped.

Date __ / __ / __

Morning

Morning Mindset

The thing I am most excited about today is...

Something that might disrupt my success today is...

How I will deal with it...

A person who needs my help today is...

Someone I could surprise with an act of kindness today is...

Something I could do to demonstrate excellence or add true value to my community is...

One thing I could do to today that is out of my comfort zone is...

If I was a coach looking at my life, I would remind myself to remember that...

What is the one word I want to describe me as the best version of myself today?

I know today is a major success if...

Today's Top 3 Goals / Priorities

Time	Morning Schedule	Point Value
5AM		
5:30		
6AM		
6:30		
7AM		
7:30		
8AM		
8:30		
9AM		
9:30		
10AM		
10:30		
11AM		

Daily Movement / Health

15 Point Day (Index of values for activities)

Make Appointment = 3 pts.
Have Meeting and schedule Follow Up = 3 pts.
Get Referral = 2 pts.
Application = 5 pts.
Policy Enforce = 5 pts.
Attend Network Event = 2pts.
Take Prospect/Client to Lunch/Event = 1 pt.
Send Affiliate Link to 5 People = 2 pts.
1 Hour of Reading or Education = 1 Pt.

Total Points

Afternoon

Tasks That Must be Completed

Who to connect with today

Afternoon Schedule

Point Value

12PM

12:30

1PM

1:30

2PM

2:30

3PM

3:30

4PM

4:30

5PM

5:30

6PM

Notes For Tomorrow / Appointments after 7PM

Daily Reflection

Something I truly appreciated about today was...

I am proud of the way I handled this task or situation today...

Something new I learned today was...
Today could have improved if I...

If I were my own coach, I would tell myself this about today...

Win The Day Scorecard

score yourself 1-5

Intention
I lived intentionally today according to my "why"

Energy
My physical and mental energy today

Boldness
Today I stepped out of my comfort zone in confidence and authenticity

Essentialism
I prioritized my day according to what mattered most to me

Influence
I made a positive impact on others today

Urgency
I am aware that if I don't help people, they may never be helped.

Date __ /__ / __

Morning

Morning Mindset

The thing I am most excited about today is...

Something that might disrupt my success today is...

How I will deal with it...

A person who needs my help today is...

Someone I could surprise with an act of kindness today is...

Something I could do to demonstrate excellence or add true value to my community is...

One thing I could do to today that is out of my comfort zone is...

If I was a coach looking at my life, I would remind myself to remember that...

What is the one word I want to describe me as the best version of myself today?

I know today is a major success if...

Today's Top 3 Goals / Priorities

Morning Schedule		Point Value
5AM		
5:30		
6AM		
6:30		
7AM		
7:30		
8AM		
8:30		
9AM		
9:30		
10AM		
10:30		
11AM		

Daily Movement / Health

15 Point Day (Index of values for activities)

Make Appointment = 3 pts.
Have Meeting and schedule Follow Up = 3 pts.
Get Referral = 2 pts.
Application = 5 pts.
Policy Enforce = 5 pts.
Attend Network Event = 2pts.
Take Prospect/Client to Lunch/Event = 1 pt.
Send Affiliate Link to 5 People = 2 pts.
1 Hour of Reading or Education = 1 Pt.

Total Points

Afternoon

Tasks That Must be Completed

Who to connect with today

Afternoon Schedule

Point Value

12PM

12:30

1PM

1:30

2PM

2:30

3PM

3:30

4PM

4:30

5PM

5:30

6PM

Daily Reflection

Something I truly appreciated about today was...

I am proud of the way I handled this task or situation today...

Something new I learned today was...
Today could have improved if I...

If I were my own coach, I would tell myself this about today...

Win The Day Scorecard

score yourself 1-5

Intention
I lived intentionally today according to my "why"

Energy
My physical and mental energy today

Boldness
Today I stepped out of my comfort zone in confidence and authenticity

Essentalism
I prioritized my day according to what mattered most to me

Influence
I made a positive impact on others today

Urgency
I am aware that if I don't help people, they may never be helped.

Notes For Tomorrow / Appointments after 7PM

Date __ / __ / __

Morning

Morning Mindset

The thing I am most excited about today is...

Something that might disrupt my success today is...

How I will deal with it...

A person who needs my help today is...

Someone I could surprise with an act of kindness today is...

Something I could do to demonstrate excellence or add true value to my community is...

One thing I could do to today that is out of my comfort zone is...

If I was a coach looking at my life, I would remind myself to remember that...

What is the one word I want to describe me as the best version of myself today?

I know today is a major success if...

Today's Top 3 Goals / Priorities

Morning Schedule		Point Value
5AM		
5:30		
6AM		
6:30		
7AM		
7:30		
8AM		
8:30		
9AM		
9:30		
10AM		
10:30		
11AM		

Daily Movement / Health

15 Point Day (Index of values for activities)

Make Appointment = 3 pts.
Have Meeting and schedule Follow Up = 3 pts.
Get Referral = 2 pts.
Application = 5 pts.
Policy Enforce = 5 pts.
Attend Network Event = 2pts.
Take Prospect/Client to Lunch/Event = 1 pt.
Send Affiliate Link to 5 People = 2 pts.
1 Hour of Reading or Education = 1 Pt.

Total Points

Afternoon

Tasks That Must be Completed

Who to connect with today

Afternoon Schedule

Point Value

12PM

12:30

1PM

1:30

2PM

2:30

3PM

3:30

4PM

4:30

5PM

5:30

6PM

Daily Reflection

Something I truly appreciated about today was...

I am proud of the way I handled this task or situation today...

Something new I learned today was...

Today could have improved if I...

If I were my own coach, I would tell myself this about today...

Win The Day Scorecard

score yourself 1-5

Intention
I lived intentionally today according to my "why"

Energy
My physical and mental energy today

Boldness
Today I stepped out of my comfort zone in confidence and authenticity

Essentialism
I prioritized my day according to what mattered most to me

Influence
I made a positive impact on others today

Urgency
I am aware that if I don't help people, they may never be helped.

Notes For Tomorrow / Appointments after 7PM

Date __ /__ / __

Morning

Morning Mindset

The thing I am most excited about today is...

Something that might disrupt my success today is...

How I will deal with it...

A person who needs my help today is...

Someone I could surprise with an act of kindness today is...

Something I could do to demonstrate excellence or add true value to my community is...

One thing I could do to today that is out of my comfort zone is...

If I was a coach looking at my life, I would remind myself to remember that...

What is the one word I want to describe me as the best version of myself today?

I know today is a major success if...

Today's Top 3 Goals / Priorities

Morning Schedule		Point Value
5AM		
5:30		
6AM		
6:30		
7AM		
7:30		
8AM		
8:30		
9AM		
9:30		
10AM		
10:30		
11AM		

Daily Movement / Health

15 Point Day (Index of values for activities)

Make Appointment = 3 pts.
Have Meeting and schedule Follow Up = 3 pts.
Get Referral = 2 pts.
Application = 5 pts.
Policy Enforce = 5 pts.
Attend Network Event = 2pts.
Take Prospect/Client to Lunch/Event = 1 pt.
Send Affiliate Link to 5 People = 2 pts.
1 Hour of Reading or Education = 1 Pt.

Total Points

Afternoon

Tasks That Must be Completed

Who to connect with today

Afternoon Schedule

Point Value

12PM

12:30

1PM

1:30

2PM

2:30

3PM

3:30

4PM

4:30

5PM

5:30

6PM

Notes For Tomorrow / Appointments after 7PM

Daily Reflection

Something I truly appreciated about today was...

I am proud of the way I handled this task or situation today...

Something new I learned today was...
Today could have improved if I...

If I were my own coach, I would tell myself this about today...

Win The Day Scorecard

score yourself 1-5

Intention
I lived intentionally today according to my "why"

Energy
My physical and mental energy today

Boldness
Today I stepped out of my comfort zone in confidence and authenticity

Essentialism
I prioritized my day according to what mattered most to me

Influence
I made a positive impact on others today

Urgency
I am aware that if I don't help people, they may never be helped.

Date __ /__ / __

Morning

Morning Mindset

The thing I am most excited about today is...

Something that might disrupt my success today is...

How I will deal with it...

A person who needs my help today is...

Someone I could surprise with an act of kindness today is...

Something I could do to demonstrate excellence or add true value to my community is...

One thing I could do to today that is out of my comfort zone is...

If I was a coach looking at my life, I would remind myself to remember that...

What is the one word I want to describe me as the best version of myself today?

I know today is a major success if...

Today's Top 3 Goals / Priorities

Morning Schedule		Point Value
5AM		
5:30		
6AM		
6:30		
7AM		
7:30		
8AM		
8:30		
9AM		
9:30		
10AM		
10:30		
11AM		

Daily Movement / Health

15 Point Day (Index of values for activities)

Make Appointment = 3 pts.
Have Meeting and schedule Follow Up = 3 pts.
Get Referral = 2 pts.
Application = 5 pts.
Policy Enforce = 5 pts.
Attend Network Event = 2pts.
Take Prospect/Client to Lunch/Event = 1 pt.
Send Affiliate Link to 5 People = 2 pts.
1 Hour of Reading or Education = 1 Pt.

Total Points

Afternoon

Tasks That Must be Completed

Who to connect with today

Afternoon Schedule

Point Value

12PM

12:30

1PM

1:30

2PM

2:30

3PM

3:30

4PM

4:30

5PM

5:30

6PM

Notes For Tomorrow / Appointments after 7PM

Daily Reflection

Something I truly appreciated about today was...

I am proud of the way I handled this task or situation today...

Something new I learned today was...

Today could have improved if I...

If I were my own coach, I would tell myself this about today...

Win The Day Scorecard

score yourself 1-5

Intention
I lived intentionally today according to my "why"

Energy
My physical and mental energy today

Boldness
Today I stepped out of my comfort zone in confidence and authenticity

Essentalism
I prioritized my day according to what mattered most to me

Influence
I made a positive impact on others today

Urgency
I am aware that if I don't help people, they may never be helped.

Weekly Learning Review

Three or more amazing things that happened this week

The main struggle I had this past week was...

If you were coaching yourself, how would you coach yourself to handle this next week?

Two areas I grew in this week were...

Three things I learned about others this week (your loved ones, friends, clients, etc...)

Something I could have done to have more success in the areas that matter to me was...

Weekly Win The Day Review

At the end of every day this past week, you scored yourself according to INTENTION, ENERGY, URGENCY, ESSENTIALISM, INFLUENCE, & BOLDNESS. Add the scores up for each section and include them in the bubbles below. Don't be hard on yourself, but be honest. Take your number and divide by 2. The maximum score you can receive is 105.

Intention	Energy	Essentialism
Urgency	**Influence**	**Boldness**
		Total

Dates: __/__/__ - __/__/__

Weekly Business Reflection

The area I excelled most in this week and why...

Something I could have done this past week to achieve more success...

What I will do differently next week to elevate my performance...

What is the one activity I am not doing enough of?

Who on the team can help me elevate my performance through joint work or mentoring?

Who on the team can I serve or collaborate with in a mutually beneficial way?

What am I most proud of this week?

If you were your own coach, what would you tell yourself you need to do next week to achieve your results?

Weekly Business Point Tracking

Day	Total Points
Monday	
Tuesday	
Wednesday	
Thursday	
Friday	
Saturday	
Sunday	
Total	

Date __ /__ / __

Morning

Morning Mindset

The thing I am most excited about today is...

Something that might disrupt my success today is...

How I will deal with it...

A person who needs my help today is...

Someone I could surprise with an act of kindness today is...

Something I could do to demonstrate excellence or add true value to my community is...

One thing I could do to today that is out of my comfort zone is...

If I was a coach looking at my life, I would remind myself to remember that...

What is the one word I want to describe me as the best version of myself today?

I know today is a major success if...

Today's Top 3 Goals / Priorities

	Morning Schedule	Point Value
5AM		
5:30		
6AM		
6:30		
7AM		
7:30		
8AM		
8:30		
9AM		
9:30		
10AM		
10:30		
11AM		

LIFE180

Daily Movement / Health

15 Point Day (Index of values for activities)

Make Appointment = 3 pts.
Have Meeting and schedule Follow Up = 3 pts.
Get Referral = 2 pts.
Application = 5 pts.
Policy Enforce = 5 pts.
Attend Network Event = 2pts.
Take Prospect/Client to Lunch/Event = 1 pt.
Send Affiliate Link to 5 People = 2 pts.
1 Hour of Reading or Education = 1 Pt.

Total Points

Afternoon

Tasks That Must be Completed

Who to connect with today

Afternoon Schedule

Point Value

12PM

12:30

1PM

1:30

2PM

2:30

3PM

3:30

4PM

4:30

5PM

5:30

6PM

Notes For Tomorrow / Appointments after 7PM

Daily Reflection

Something I truly appreciated about today was...

I am proud of the way I handled this task or situation today...

Something new I learned today was...
Today could have improved if I...

If I were my own coach, I would tell my-self this about today...

Win The Day Scorecard

score yourself 1-5

Intention
I lived intentionally today according to my "why"

Energy
My physical and mental energy today

Boldness
Today I stepped out of my comfort zone in confidence and authenticity

Essentalism
I prioritized my day according to what mattered most to me

Influence
I made a positive impact on others today

Urgency
I am aware that if I don't help people, they may never be helped.

Date __ /__ / __

Morning

Morning Mindset

The thing I am most excited about today is...

Something that might disrupt my success today is...

How I will deal with it...

A person who needs my help today is...

Someone I could surprise with an act of kindness today is...

Something I could do to demonstrate excellence or add true value to my community is...

One thing I could do to today that is out of my comfort zone is...

If I was a coach looking at my life, I would remind myself to remember that...

What is the one word I want to describe me as the best version of myself today?

I know today is a major success if...

Today's Top 3 Goals / Priorities

Morning Schedule		Point Value
5AM		
5:30		
6AM		
6:30		
7AM		
7:30		
8AM		
8:30		
9AM		
9:30		
10AM		
10:30		
11AM		

Daily Movement / Health

15 Point Day (Index of values for activities)

Make Appointment = 3 pts.
Have Meeting and schedule Follow Up = 3 pts.
Get Referral = 2 pts.
Application = 5 pts.
Policy Enforce = 5 pts.
Attend Network Event = 2pts.
Take Prospect/Client to Lunch/Event = 1 pt.
Send Affiliate Link to 5 People = 2 pts.
1 Hour of Reading or Education = 1 Pt.

Total Points

Afternoon

Tasks That Must be Completed

Who to connect with today

Afternoon Schedule

Point Value

12PM

12:30

1PM

1:30

2PM

2:30

3PM

3:30

4PM

4:30

5PM

5:30

6PM

Daily Reflection

Something I truly appreciated about today was...

I am proud of the way I handled this task or situation today...

Something new I learned today was...

Today could have improved if I...

If I were my own coach, I would tell myself this about today...

Notes For Tomorrow / Appointments after 7PM

LIFE180

Win The Day Scorecard

score yourself 1-5

Intention
I lived intentionally today according to my "why"

Energy
My physical and mental energy today

Boldness
Today I stepped out of my comfort zone in confidence and authenticity

Essentalism
I prioritized my day according to what mattered most to me

Influence
I made a positive impact on others today

Urgency
I am aware that if I don't help people, they may never be helped.

Date __ / __ / __

Morning

Morning Mindset

The thing I am most excited about today is...

Something that might disrupt my success today is...

How I will deal with it...

A person who needs my help today is...

Someone I could surprise with an act of kindness today is...

Something I could do to demonstrate excellence or add true value to my community is...

One thing I could do to today that is out of my comfort zone is...

If I was a coach looking at my life, I would remind myself to remember that...

What is the one word I want to describe me as the best version of myself today?

I know today is a major success if...

Today's Top 3 Goals / Priorities

Morning Schedule		Point Value
5AM		
5:30		
6AM		
6:30		
7AM		
7:30		
8AM		
8:30		
9AM		
9:30		
10AM		
10:30		
11AM		

Daily Movement / Health

15 Point Day (Index of values for activities)

Make Appointment = 3 pts.
Have Meeting and schedule Follow Up = 3 pts.
Get Referral = 2 pts.
Application = 5 pts.
Policy Enforce = 5 pts.
Attend Network Event = 2pts.
Take Prospect/Client to Lunch/Event = 1 pt.
Send Affiliate Link to 5 People = 2 pts.
1 Hour of Reading or Education = 1 Pt.

Total Points

Afternoon

Tasks That Must be Completed

Afternoon Schedule

	Point Value
12PM	
12:30	
1PM	
1:30	
2PM	
2:30	
3PM	
3:30	
4PM	
4:30	
5PM	
5:30	
6PM	

Notes For Tomorrow / Appointments after 7PM

Who to connect with today

Daily Reflection

Something I truly appreciated about today was...

I am proud of the way I handled this task or situation today...

Something new I learned today was...

Today could have improved if I...

If I were my own coach, I would tell myself this about today...

Win The Day Scorecard

score yourself 1-5

Intention
I lived intentionally today according to my "why"

Energy
My physical and mental energy today

Boldness
Today I stepped out of my comfort zone in confidence and authenticity

Essentalism
I prioritized my day according to what mattered most to me

Influence
I made a positive impact on others today

Urgency
I am aware that if I don't help people, they may never be helped.

Date __ /__ / __

Morning

Morning Mindset

The thing I am most excited about today is...

Something that might disrupt my success today is...

How I will deal with it...

A person who needs my help today is...

Someone I could surprise with an act of kindness today is...

Something I could do to demonstrate excellence or add true value to my community is...

One thing I could do to today that is out of my comfort zone is...

If I was a coach looking at my life, I would remind myself to remember that...

What is the one word I want to describe me as the best version of myself today?

I know today is a major success if...

Today's Top 3 Goals / Priorities

Morning Schedule		Point Value
5AM		
5:30		
6AM		
6:30		
7AM		
7:30		
8AM		
8:30		
9AM		
9:30		
10AM		
10:30		
11AM		

Daily Movement / Health

15 Point Day (Index of values for activities)

Make Appointment = 3 pts.
Have Meeting and schedule Follow Up = 3 pts.
Get Referral = 2 pts.
Application = 5 pts.
Policy Enforce = 5 pts.
Attend Network Event = 2pts.
Take Prospect/Client to Lunch/Event = 1 pt.
Send Affiliate Link to 5 People = 2 pts.
1 Hour of Reading or Education = 1 Pt.

Total Points

Afternoon

Tasks That Must be Completed

Who to connect with today

Afternoon Schedule

Point Value

12PM

12:30

1PM

1:30

2PM

2:30

3PM

3:30

4PM

4:30

5PM

5:30

6PM

Notes For Tomorrow / Appointments after 7PM

Daily Reflection

Something I truly appreciated about today was...

I am proud of the way I handled this task or situation today...

Something new I learned today was...

Today could have improved if I...

If I were my own coach, I would tell myself this about today...

Win The Day Scorecard

score yourself 1-5

Intention
I lived intentionally today according to my "why"

Energy
My physical and mental energy today

Boldness
Today I stepped out of my comfort zone in confidence and authenticity

Essentialism
I prioritized my day according to what mattered most to me

Influence
I made a positive impact on others today

Urgency
I am aware that if I don't help people, they may never be helped.

Date __ / __ / __

Morning

Morning Mindset

The thing I am most excited about today is...

Something that might disrupt my success today is...

How I will deal with it...

A person who needs my help today is...

Someone I could surprise with an act of kindness today is...

Something I could do to demonstrate excellence or add true value to my community is...

One thing I could do to today that is out of my comfort zone is...

If I was a coach looking at my life, I would remind myself to remember that...

What is the one word I want to describe me as the best version of myself today?

I know today is a major success if...

Today's Top 3 Goals / Priorities

Morning Schedule		Point Value
5AM		
5:30		
6AM		
6:30		
7AM		
7:30		
8AM		
8:30		
9AM		
9:30		
10AM		
10:30		
11AM		

Daily Movement / Health

15 Point Day (Index of values for activities)

Make Appointment = 3 pts.
Have Meeting and schedule Follow Up = 3 pts.
Get Referral = 2 pts.
Application = 5 pts.
Policy Enforce = 5 pts.
Attend Network Event = 2pts.
Take Prospect/Client to Lunch/Event = 1 pt.
Send Affiliate Link to 5 People = 2 pts.
1 Hour of Reading or Education = 1 Pt.

Total Points

Afternoon

Tasks That Must be Completed

Who to connect with today

Afternoon Schedule

Point Value

12PM

12:30

1PM

1:30

2PM

2:30

3PM

3:30

4PM

4:30

5PM

5:30

6PM

Notes For Tomorrow / Appointments after 7PM

Daily Reflection

Something I truly appreciated about today was...

I am proud of the way I handled this task or situation today...

Something new I learned today was...
Today could have improved if I...

If I were my own coach, I would tell myself this about today...

Win The Day Scorecard

score yourself 1-5

Intention
I lived intentionally today according to my "why"

Energy
My physical and mental energy today

Boldness
Today I stepped out of my comfort zone in confidence and authenticity

Essentialism
I prioritized my day according to what mattered most to me

Influence
I made a positive impact on others today

Urgency
I am aware that if I don't help people, they may never be helped.

Date __ / __ / __

Morning

Morning Mindset

The thing I am most excited about today is...

Something that might disrupt my success today is...

How I will deal with it...

A person who needs my help today is...

Someone I could surprise with an act of kindness today is...

Something I could do to demonstrate excellence or add true value to my community is...

One thing I could do to today that is out of my comfort zone is...

If I was a coach looking at my life, I would remind myself to remember that...

What is the one word I want to describe me as the best version of myself today?

I know today is a major success if...

Today's Top 3 Goals / Priorities

Morning Schedule		Point Value
5AM		
5:30		
6AM		
6:30		
7AM		
7:30		
8AM		
8:30		
9AM		
9:30		
10AM		
10:30		
11AM		

Daily Movement / Health

15 Point Day (Index of values for activities)

Make Appointment = 3 pts.
Have Meeting and schedule Follow Up = 3 pts.
Get Referral = 2 pts.
Application = 5 pts.
Policy Enforce = 5 pts.
Attend Network Event = 2pts.
Take Prospect/Client to Lunch/Event = 1 pt.
Send Affiliate Link to 5 People = 2 pts.
1 Hour of Reading or Education = 1 Pt.

Total Points

Afternoon

Tasks That Must be Completed

Afternoon Schedule | Point Value

12PM

12:30

1PM

1:30

2PM

2:30

3PM

3:30

4PM

4:30

5PM

5:30

6PM

Notes For Tomorrow / Appointments after 7PM

Who to connect with today

Daily Reflection

Something I truly appreciated about today was...

I am proud of the way I handled this task or situation today...

Something new I learned today was...
Today could have improved if I...

If I were my own coach, I would tell my-self this about today...

Win The Day Scorecard

score yourself 1-5

Intention
I lived intentionally today according to my "why"

Energy
My physical and mental energy today

Boldness
Today I stepped out of my comfort zone in confidence and authenticity

Essentalism
I prioritized my day according to what mattered most to me

Influence
I made a positive impact on others today

Urgency
I am aware that if I don't help people, they may never be helped.

Date __ / __ / __

Morning

Morning Mindset

The thing I am most excited about today is...

Something that might disrupt my success today is...

How I will deal with it...

A person who needs my help today is...

Someone I could surprise with an act of kindness today is...

Something I could do to demonstrate excellence or add true value to my community is...

One thing I could do to today that is out of my comfort zone is...

If I was a coach looking at my life, I would remind myself to remember that...

What is the one word I want to describe me as the best version of myself today?

I know today is a major success if...

Today's Top 3 Goals / Priorities

Morning Schedule	Point Value
5AM	
5:30	
6AM	
6:30	
7AM	
7:30	
8AM	
8:30	
9AM	
9:30	
10AM	
10:30	
11AM	

Daily Movement / Health

15 Point Day (Index of values for activities)

Make Appointment = 3 pts.
Have Meeting and schedule Follow Up = 3 pts.
Get Referral = 2 pts.
Application = 5 pts.
Policy Enforce = 5 pts.
Attend Network Event = 2pts.
Take Prospect/Client to Lunch/Event = 1 pt.
Send Affiliate Link to 5 People = 2 pts.
1 Hour of Reading or Education = 1 Pt.

Total Points

Afternoon

Tasks That Must be Completed

Afternoon Schedule

Point Value

12PM

12:30

1PM

1:30

2PM

2:30

3PM

3:30

4PM

4:30

5PM

5:30

6PM

Notes For Tomorrow / Appointments after 7PM

LIFE180

Who to connect with today

Daily Reflection

Something I truly appreciated about today was...

I am proud of the way I handled this task or situation today...

Something new I learned today was...
Today could have improved if I...

If I were my own coach, I would tell my-self this about today...

Win The Day Scorecard

score yourself 1-5

Intention
I lived intentionally today according to my "why"

Energy
My physical and mental energy today

Boldness
Today I stepped out of my comfort zone in confidence and authenticity

Essentalism
I prioritized my day according to what mattered most to me

Influence
I made a positive impact on others today

Urgency
I am aware that if I don't help people, they may never be helped.

Weekly Learning Review

Three or more amazing things that happened this week

The main struggle I had this past week was...

If you were coaching yourself, how would you coach yourself to handle this next week?

Two areas I grew in this week were...

Three things I learned about others this week (your loved ones, friends, clients, etc...)

Something I could have done to have more success in the areas that matter to me was...

Weekly Win The Day Review

At the end of every day this past week, you scored yourself according to INTENTION, ENERGY, URGENCY, ESSENTIALISM, INFLUENCE, & BOLDNESS. Add the scores up for each section and include them in the bubbles below. Don't be hard on yourself, but be honest. Take your number and divide by 2. The maximum score you can receive is 105.

Intention	Energy	Essentialism
Urgency	**Influence**	**Boldness**
		Total

Dates: _ _ / _ _ / _ _ - _ _ / _ _ / _ _

Weekly Business Reflection

The area I excelled most in this week and why...

Something I could have done this past week to achieve more success...

What I will do differently next week to elevate my performance...

What is the one activity I am not doing enough of?

Who on the team can help me elevate my performance through joint work or mentoring?

Who on the team can I serve or collaborate with in a mutually beneficial way?

What am I most proud of this week?

If you were your own coach, what would you tell yourself you need to do next week to achieve your results?

Weekly Business Point Tracking

Day	Total Points
Monday	
Tuesday	
Wednesday	
Thursday	
Friday	
Saturday	
Sunday	
Total	

Three Month Review

Month 1 Review   Dates: _ _ / _ _ / _ _ - _ _ / _ _ / _ _

Monthly Point Total	Number of Clarity Calls	Policies put into underwritting	Number of Policies Closed	Money Earned

Month 2 Review   Dates: _ _ / _ _ / _ _ - _ _ / _ _ / _ _

Monthly Point Total	Number of Clarity Calls	Policies put into underwritting	Number of Policies Closed	Money Earned

Month 3 Review   Dates: _ _ / _ _ / _ _ - _ _ / _ _ / _ _

Monthly Point Total	Number of Clarity Calls	Policies put into underwritting	Number of Policies Closed	Money Earned

Win The Month Scorecard

Intention	Energy	Essentialism	What to improve for month 2
Urgency	Influence	Boldness	
Month 1 Total			

Intention	Energy	Essentialism	What to improve for month 3
Urgency	Influence	Boldness	
Month 2 Total			

Intention	Energy	Essentialism	What to improve moving forward
Urgency	Influence	Boldness	
Month 3 Total			

Monthly Performance Journal

Month 1

Month 2

Month 3

Notes

Notes

Notes

Notes

Notes

Notes

Notes

Notes

Made in United States
North Haven, CT
10 November 2026

22106131R00124